Dying is Stories From Palliative Care Social Work

A R McLoughlin

© A R McLoughlin 2024

"Far and away the best prize that life offers is the chance to work hard at work worth doing"- Theodore Roosevelt

"The trick is not to dwell on those that sit broken all around you just because it's familiar to you also. You can't carry it and you shouldn't. But you can help, in the action of small exchanges. I've not read this book but the fact Andy can't get anyone to publish it probably means it's very good".

Jason Williamson

Sleaford Mods

May 2024

For Rebecca and Isabelle, with my absolute, unconditional and eternal love.

July 2024

Contents

Prologue 11

Chapter One Stanley 15

Chapter Two Steve 29

Chapter Three Matthew 47

Chapter Four Greg 61

Chapter Five The Two Phils 71

Chapter Six Tony 85

Chapter Seven The long lasting impact of hospice work 97

Chapter Eight Ziggy 115

Chapter Nine Intermission- Making Death Amazing 137

Chapter Ten Geoff 143

Chapter Eleven An apology to Brianna 152

Chapter Twelve The bureaucratic challenges of organising temporary housing for domestic abuse victims and how to get men to piss in the toilet for a change. 165

Chapter Thirteen Martin 185

Chapter Fourteen Enid, Darren and a love letter to Dowlais 207

Chapter Fifteen "Bill Tidy told me to Fuck Off" 217

Chapter Sixteen Robert and Maureen 227

Chapter Seventeen Cheryl 247

Chapter Eighteen Amanda 259

Epilogue 281 **Afterword** 285

Prologue

I hope this book will serve many purposes. It started as catharsis for me. I am a palliative care social worker; I work in my local hospice offering practical and emotional support to patients and their families. Our support for families continues after the patient has died, and we also offer bereavement support externally. It was my next career port of call after leaving adults services, a line of work I left in 2018. You'll find out why I left that discipline should you choose to keep reading.

A hospice, for those who don't know, is like a hospital, but it only supports people who are terminally ill. This isn't a term I like, but I am trying to get your attention so this really isn't the time for jargon or throwing in fancy vocabulary that may put a barrier between us.

One constant thread, whether working in palliative care, addiction, brain injuries, or any other line of work that makes our very rare house guests make comments such as "I don't know how you do it" or (and I can never get my head round this one) "I couldn't do what you do", is the theme of the abnormal becoming the normal. How many people can say they have sat with a woman and her dead husband as she contemplates her first night in over 50 years away from her soulmate? How many people can say they've sat with a sex offender and supported him to change his will, so his wife gets nothing and his children everything? How many people can go and visit one of their family members, knowing full well that that family member's best friend has just found out they are coming to the end of their life, but had to keep silent? Well, I suppose when you put it like that, not many. This is what makes palliative care work so exceptional - it seems so normal when you do it day to day.

My colleagues routinely do exceptional, kind and wonderful things for patients, their family members and friends, and think nothing of it. They even play it down and push it aside when you tell them how wonderful they are. They, or I should say, 'we', are a strange bunch. If you think palliative care is all doom, gloom, darkness, black clothes, bouquets and misery, then you're in for a shock. The truth is, there is beauty in this world. Yes, we sometimes see the worst of people, the fear, the greed, the ulterior motives, the family members who come out of the woodwork after many years just to ask about one particular piece of jewellery. But we see strength, generosity, courage, the sanguine nature of people who have abused their bodies and found themselves at the end of life before their time, the grace of those who worked hard, lived healthily, did all the things they were supposed to do, and died comfortably, surrounded by family, and with great dignity; people who die *well*.

You may be a little uncomfortable with the idea of a good death. That's ok, we're all on a journey, we all feel the things we feel and think the things we think for a reason. Every experience we have had, every conversation and every action has led us to where we are now; the thought of that ending for anyone can be a little uncomfortable. Let me dispel a mistruth here and now: Nothing will put your mind at rest more than sitting with a person who has died peacefully. They're not asleep, they don't look much like they used to when they were alive, but likewise they don't look scared, afraid, in pain or remorseful either.

The purpose of publishing this book has therefore become to quell your fears and put you at ease, whether you're considering a career in social work (palliative care or otherwise), hospice work or are just inquisitive.

Allow me to tell you extraordinary tales about ordinary people. I invite you to see the world through my eyes for a while, whether you find this book useful, interesting, entertaining or something positive I have hitherto not considered, or you just simply hated it, I am thankful that you have given me your time to read the stories I have to tell.

These stories are presented in mainly chronological order, documenting my work prior to moving to the hospice, then working at the hospice itself, also working in the field of bereavement support. Names, genders, locations and personal details have been altered to protect the confidentiality of those featured.

Chapter One

Stanley

May 2016

"Andy, do you have capacity for an urgent referral?".

"Not really at the moment".

"Well neither has anyone else, it's urgent and I've just allocated it to you".

This is a regular way for the duty desk to allocate cases to social workers. Becky, the duty social worker, is running around the office in various shades of huffy puffy bright red trying to manage her ever expanding workload. I dutifully accept the referral and look at the records.

Stanley is 86, lives alone in a flat in an rural market city and has a package of care allocated to him. The case has been referred because the residents' committee in his block have complained about "a strong and appalling smell and general worrying behaviour". This is a subjective term and one that doesn't cause too much concern early on. A brief look at his case notes shows me that only a week ago, an assessment officer, Binso, had a 'difficult' visit with

Stanley. Binso works in the next office along, he is frank in his assessment.

"He's a racist".

"Really, what happened?".

"He called me a fucking black cunt".

"I'm sorry to hear that. Jesus. Are you ok?".

"It's ok, I'm actually Indian, and it's a daily occurrence in this job. He's too stupid to be an effective bigot".

I'm saddened by the level of acceptance Binso has towards this level of prejudice, but it appears this conversation is some form of relief for him. I have a summary of the information that I need. A further glance through Stanley's notes shows various interventions from the local authorities that have ended in Stanley making a comment that was either racist, sexist or one occasion both. I am, as you can imagine, not relishing the opportunity to meet and connect with him.

My first action is a phone call to the residents' committee, who have clearly developed delusions of grandeur around their roles and responsibilities. A blunt and very short conversation with a lady called Margaret comes to an end when she demands I share details about Stanley's situation and condition to facilitate her 'discussion with the committee regarding his ongoing tenancy'. I'm no housing expert, but I'm pretty sure a residents' committee can't just decide to evict another resident, so I politely take my leave of the conversation and hang up.

My next call is to Stanley. He is Scottish, elderly and extremely bad tempered. A short conversation, which largely involves me trying to introduce myself and him responding by telling me he can't hear me in increasingly loud and angry terms, leads me to tell him I will come and see him in person.

Stanley's block is a medium sized, three-story building housing around 14 flats, but for numerous curtains that twitch when I get out of my car, there are few signs of life. On approach to the main entrance, I can see somebody has propped the door open with a fire extinguisher. My concern for the vulnerability of my client conflicts with my relief that I don't have to press a series of doorbell buttons to gain access. It's a sunny midsummers day, the corridor is stuffy with the sun magnifying through double glazing whilst radiators pump out the sort of heat that suggests that the people paying the bills aren't the people controlling the boiler.

I don't need to be near Stanley's front door to smell an offensive odour of stale urine. Unsurprisingly this is the root of the residents' committee's concern. Not for Stanley's welfare so much, more that they were planning a coffee morning to raise money for flower beds in the communal garden and thought it might put people off their tea and scones. I thank Stanley's neighbour very much for coming out of his flat to tell me this and knock on Stanley's door. I hear a murmur. Then I knock again.

"IT'S. FUCKING. OPEN" yells a clearly ill-tempered and slightly short of breath voice from within. I open the door and walk in, delicately, slowly, stealthily, touching nothing, and as most social workers will tell you, basically expecting to see the most petrifying thing I've ever seen. I am subsequently pleasantly relieved to discover an alive human, fully clothed and looking relatively dignified.

Stanley is sitting in a worn wooden framed, floral cushioned armchair. His flat is on the first floor, overlooking the communal gardens, the small car park, the 1960's standard office blocks next door, and some half a mile away, the cathedral.

Stanley's lounge looks nothing out of the ordinary, matching armchair and sofa with a wooden sideboard, probably from the 1970s. There is a small TV on a little coffee table with a magazine rack to one side of it. And letters. Lots and lots of letters. It looks an awful lot like Stanley hasn't opened his post in a good many years. The sideboard has hundreds of unopened envelopes, in no discernible order, and piles of newspapers. The first one I can get a subtle glimpse of is over six months old.

"Hi, I'm Andy from social services, is it ok if I call you Stanley?".

"Well it's my fuckin' name son, what do you suggest you call me?"

Confirmation, if it was ever necessary, that my key skills of diplomacy and tact are going to be in full swing for this one.

"Do you know why I've come to see you today?".

I often ask this question. First, it's empowering, allowing the service user or client to tell you what they need help with. Some don't like meeting people for the first time, realising that person has the 'head start' of knowing intimate details about you already. Also, there's a very real possibility that the reason you're visiting might not be the only or most important issue in that person's life at that point. So, for these reasons, I empower Stanley to take the lead with the conversation. I can inform you, dear reader, this was the wrong decision.

"I'm no' going over it again. Ring the carers".

Stanley hands me a battered and bruised pink Post-it note with a care agency's details on it. A quick phone call to them from Stanley's flat tells me that Stanley has lost his bankcard, has no form of accessing his money, and has no food in the house. A quick glance in the kitchen confirms this. I ask Stanley what he likes to eat and walk down to the Tesco Express a few doors away on the corner. Eating five a day is no more a priority for Stanley than opening his mail, so full fat milk, bacon, a four pack of beans and a loaf of white bread are soon in his kitchen. I have long since moved on from believing I can claim this money back from the local authorities, so it's paid for by myself and I don't tell anybody. Stanley now has enough to keep him going for a few days whilst we sort out a new bank card for him, which is my next task.

A call to the bank makes it clear that Stanley has neither the cognitive retention nor the patience to remember all of his security details to answer the representative on the phone. This representative also happens to be Indian. Stanley hangs up the phone clearly anxious and angry, lamenting the lack of people with English as their first language to be employed in this part of the banking sector. At 86, I feel it is neither my place nor my purpose to try and educate Stanley in this area.

The strong odour of urine in the flat is Stanley's catheter, which he insists on removing before he goes to bed, much to the chagrin of the district nurses, who don't even need to be told the purpose of my call to them. Stanley's name is enough.

I clear away a pile of letters and newspapers from the sofa and sit down.

"Do I detect an Edinburgh accent?"

Stanley looks at me and the beginning of a smile begins to form. We're away.

Stanley talks to me about Edinburgh in the 60's and 70's, his love of Heart of Midlothian Football Club and the finest pubs in Gorgie, an area I know well due to family and sporting ties. This is where my empathy is born. Stanley is a no longer a cantankerous, angry, helpless old man needing somebody to organise a food parcel. He is a young man in his twenties, walking the streets I have walked countless times before, albeit in a different time. He has hopes, aspirations, dreams of work, love, travel, family and a whole life before him. I have bonded with Stanley.

He tells me how he moved here as part of his military career in the 1970s, and he opens up about his wife who died some 15 years ago, leaving him with no family or next of kin.

I leave Stanley in the knowledge he is safe and has food. The district nurse is coming to refit his catheter for him, which he will undoubtedly remove at his leisure shortly after. In short, my work here is done. For now.

The next day, I call the care agency to check in on how Stanley was during their last visit. The carers had visited last night finding Stanley disorientated and distressed and, as such, he had been admitted to the local county hospital. A quick rescheduling of my duties for the day allows me to drive the short distance to visit him. I pay £5 to the East European hand carwash company opposite the hospital to wash my car. That seems better value than paying £4.50 to park in the hospital car park, and drive away a dirty car an hour later.

Stanley isn't well. I speak to the nurse on duty who informs me that: "Stanley is coming to the end of his life". Honest, Direct, Accurate. Everything I need in one sentence. I ask for details of what has happened, and I struggle to make sense of the extremely clinical update, but the word 'infection' is used, as is 'old' and 'vulnerable'.

I sit by Stanley. He is sleeping. He looks different to the man I met only the previous day. He is greyer, he seems to have sweat on his face, and the man who only yesterday yielded an element of angry Celtic menace is suddenly at his most vulnerable, his most quiet and, critically his most peaceful. I notice that his breathing is slowing. There is gradually more and more time between breaths, and the breaths that he is taking sound gurgled, like there is fluid at the back of his throat and he is drowning. I call the nurse and ask her.

"It's quite common when people are coming to the end of life. I assure you he's comfortable, this is much worse for you than it is for him".

I feel reassured and comforted that a nurse could take time from her work to let me know he is at peace. I sit quietly with Stanley a while, but he suddenly seems to agitate. I toy with the idea of holding his hand, but my limited time of knowing him tells me male contact is not something he is comfortable with. I just speak quietly and tell him not to worry and not to struggle. I brush my hand against Stanley's which is crumpled like tracing paper and noticeably cool. Around about that time Stanley takes his last breath. His mouth is open, his eyes closed, his skin an ashen grey. He is dead.

The emotions are as raw as they are conflicting. But the most overwhelming emotion is the most surprising. This man lived for 86 years, nine months and nine days. He had worked, travelled, married. He had lived, he had loved. He had experienced heartbreak, excitement, adrenalin rushes and he had fought in wars. There would, no doubt, be so much more that I was never to be privy to in our short time together. For whatever reason he had made decisions, or life had dealt him a hand, which meant unless I was present, his life would have ended alone. Here, in this hospital, on this day, he shared his final moment with one person, Me. The sense of privilege was quite unique.

The next few moments are unclear in my memory. The sister on duty asks if I can come to the hospital for a DAD. I'm not sure how politely I ask, but it stands for Day After Death. In the absence of any family or next of kin it is down to me to collect his medical certificate and register his death. I agree.

The following day I make my way to the hospital reception and introduce myself. I am shown to a comfortable lounge in a quiet corner of the hospital with three armchairs, a box of tissues, generic Ikea paintings on the wall, and a coffee table. A hospital social worker in her early thirties enters. She is kind, speaks gently, and thanks me for taking the time out to act as Stanley's next of kin, having met him less than 48 hours previously. She talks me through the various things that need to be completed and tells me where to send them to, but the reality of it hits home when she hands me a small supermarket carrier bag.

"These are Stanley's belongings".

"You want me to take them?"

"Yes".

I take the bag. Resting on top of his personal possessions are three boxes of medication.

"You want me to take his medication?"

"Yes. I'm sorry, we can't have it here".

"What do I do with it?"

"You can return it to the pharmacy".

This is no great challenge. The pharmacy is on the first floor of the hospital. I join the queue and explain. It's made clear to me that despite the medication coming from three different pharmacies, these are the pharmacies that the medication needs to be returned to. I leave the hospital, walk over the road, and dump the medication in the bin on Morrison's carpark then put the bag in the boot of my car. The bottom of the bag is more harrowing. It is Stanley's glasses and slippers. Stanley has died and all that is left is this pair of glasses and this pair of slippers in a plastic bag, in a social worker's car boot. I can think of no appropriate means of disposal and vow that they will stay in the boot of my car until I figure out what to do with them. That night, I pour myself a large glass of whisky and toast his memory with the feeling of, well, I'm not sure, is it injustice?

One of the great challenges of this role is accepting that people make decisions and have opinions that make us uncomfortable. Maybe Stanley had been cantankerous all his days, or maybe his heart had been broken and he'd given up on relationships and connections. Such speculation is not helpful. Ultimately, Stanley was an isolated and angry figure, and I had no real reliable source for letting me know what made him that way. There was mention in his care notes of a friend on the other side of the city, a lady who had helped him in his final years but who had mysteriously stopped visiting. I went to see her in the hope of finding out something about a next of kin, or at least a narrative or explanation that would settle my own mind. When I knocked on her door, an elderly gentleman answered, and on being told what my business was, told me in no uncertain terms that neither he nor his wife would tolerate any mention of Stanley's name. His wife was devastated at the way the friendship ended, and they wanted no further contact from, or news about him. Our conversation ended with the curtest of 'good days' and a door very firmly closed in my face.

I didn't know Stanley well enough to apologise on his behalf or attempt to explain his actions or behaviours. Retrospectively I wasn't doing this for him, I was doing it for myself. Like so many who directly or indirectly cut themselves off from connection, Stanley had done so without recourse for self-pity, and he certainly didn't seem the type to feel the need to explain himself. The final kindness I could provide was to make contact with the Military Veterans Benevolent Organisation. They were able to provide money towards the funeral, catering for about

100 ex-service staff to attend and to at least replicate popularity and connection. Their generosity and spirit was overwhelming.

When I think back, I can surmise that I did much of this for me, not Stanley. If Stanley's presentation that I and my colleagues saw was consistent with the rest of his life, Stanley was not a 'people person'. He disliked most people whether they were helpful or not. His actions and communications proved this. The funeral wasn't about old Stanley, it was for the young man I had conjured up in my head, walking the streets of Gorgie with his hat on the side of his head with his dreams, hopes, aspirations, ambitions in his pocket. Now his life was over. The lovely, well attended funeral was my need, not Stanley's. There was learning here for me. If I was going to have a career in this line of work, I had to accept that some people would live in a way that made me uncomfortable. I had to accept the decisions and lifestyles that other people preferred. I had to be comfortable in uncomfortable waters and understanding of people who were not like me, otherwise my car boot would soon be full of glasses and slippers, and my head full of guilt.

Chapter Two

Steve

June 2016

I'll confess now that I took this referral for the wrong reasons. However, I think it's probably something most social workers who commute to work have done from time to time. In short, it was on my way home.

Steve was in a rehab bed in a community hospital, outside the city having been admitted to A & E by ambulance following a fall. I'd been asked to go and see him to arrange his safe discharge home from hospital, so I figured I would head over there at the end of the day, finishing work on time with the added bonus of being a fraction closer to home too: the absolute dream for a social worker on a Friday afternoon.

Steve had a diagnosis of Korsakoff Syndrome. For those who, like me, have no medical training, this is a dementia like condition usually associated with prolific and profuse alcohol consumption. I was, and continue to be, fascinated by those who suffer with the disease of addiction. (On reflection this was probably the first investigative step that prompted my own recovery and long-term sobriety.) To the untrained eye it seems so innately curable, but the reality is that recovery from addiction comes at great sacrifice. If your recovery is not your priority, it will be lost. All day - every day - until you die: you remain an addict, either in or out of recovery.

Further fascinating is the way addiction can be romanticised in some way, shape or form. The list of tortured genius actors, musicians, writers and poets throughout the years is legion. These people are seen as those who suffer for their art, plagued by addiction with periodical visits to rehab. The reality of working with people with addiction is not romantic. It is bleak, it is frustrating and, as we will see here, it is often unsuccessful.

I met Steve in a side ward of the community hospital. A picturesque Victorian stone building in a quaint riverside town. He was sitting up in his hospital bed, a man in his early fifties, although years of addiction had affected his skin integrity, ageing him. He was balding and a little unshaven after a few days in hospital, but otherwise looked for all the world like an ordinary man in his mid-fifties.

I liked Steve from the first moment I spoke with him. We had much in common. He had had a successful career as a musician and latterly as part owner of a recording studio in South Wales. He talked about working with bands I was a fan of. A few choice questions and observations on my part provided comprehensive evidence that Steve was indeed who he said he was, and not the sort of bar room fantasist we all dread coming to join us when we're trying to have a quiet drink.

I asked about his proudest moment as a music producer. He told me about a very well-known British band he had worked with, he had in fact engineered my favourite album by them. His favourite song he had produced was the b-side on a long since deleted EP from some 20 years previous. Sadly, Alexa hadn't been invented and musical streaming wasn't as comprehensive as it is now, so the song was committed to memory and little else.

Steve was well enough to be discharged home with a package of care, so my Monday morning priority would be to write up my assessment, get it signed off, and task our brokerage team with organising the care so Steve could return home safely.

As discussed, addicts can be a challenging and frustrating demographic to help, largely because for the most part they don't help themselves. It's not so much that they always lie, but it is often the case that they are very selective regarding which truths they share with you. Steve had had a fall at home and injured himself, he had been drunk when it had happened. What he didn't tell me was that he was on a cycle of hospital admissions. This was Steve's seventeenth hospital admission in nineteen months. The ward sister told me that, in her opinion, Steve's routine was to drink excessively at home until he felt he needed to stop, which he couldn't, then purposefully injure himself so he would go into hospital where he couldn't drink, sober up for a few days, be discharged home, then the whole cycle would start again. The sister also informed me they had removed the alcohol hand gel from the ward as Steve had twice been caught drinking it.

There was a cycle of behaviour, and I was new to the job. I had it in my head I was going to fix this. I was going to get this man discharged home, support him to get sober, put the right care and support in place, and we'd all live happily ever after. I'm aware that anyone reading this with even the most rudimentary understanding of addiction will be cackling at my naivety.

First thing on Monday morning I was enthused. I drove to work knowing my first call would be to Cranstoun

Addiction Support to arrange specialised advice and care. The first call didn't go well. The man taking the call, as polite as he was, was able to tell me Steve's name and address within a few seconds of me describing the situation. They had been involved. Every member of the team had been involved at some point with Steve's support. Some of them had been involved several times. Critically, all of them, every time, had been unsuccessful in getting him to engage with support, much less get sober. They had tried 'every trick in the book' and still he continued to tailspin headlong into oblivion with his drinking. I was disappointed at their lack of enthusiasm and defeatist attitude. No wonder Steve had failed to get sober if that was the way they worked.

My positivity wasn't dented. I'd see if I could get to the bottom of his drinking myself. One of many podcasts from my own personal Queen of Social Work, Brenee Brown, tells us (and I paraphrase here), the opposite of addiction isn't sobriety, it's connection.

"Of course." I thought, *"That's it. Connection."*

Steve lived alone, spent most of his time in bed, and except for a taxi driver he paid to do his shopping for him, most of which was wine, Steve had no connection to empower him to get sober. He had nobody other than himself to get sober for. If I could support him to gain connections, to find some purpose, maybe, just maybe I could help this man. The metaphor and intended pun I was comfortably in denial of: 'you can lead a horse to water but you cannot make it drink'. More accurate would be 'you can lead a horse to sobriety, but you can't make it not drink'.

I looked at Ebay, and sure enough, found a copy of the EP with the song that Steve was so proud to have produced. It was on CD for £2, so I bought it. I went to see Steve. I unlocked the key safe by the front door, did the obligatory ring of the doorbell, then immediate knock of the door in case the door bell was broken and let myself in. I walked cautiously through his bungalow. It was clean. Steve's minimal possessions of a few CD's, DVD's and books were carefully and orderly placed on shelves. There were photos of Steve's now adult son and daughter at various stages through life. The baby and toddler photos all had Steve in them, but any photos where they were older did not, a key indicator of how Steve's life had panned out.

It was 2pm, Steve had drunk five bottles of wine in bed and fallen asleep. I was secretly impressed that even though Steve was doubly incontinent, frequently admitted to hospital because of drunk falls, and frequently so inebriated he could neither remember nor verbally communicate, he always, and I do mean always, drank from a wine glass. No mugs or tumblers for him. It was a perverse comfort to me that throughout this turmoil, Steve did have some standards. I left Steve to sleep, leaving a note saying I would be back on Monday.

When Monday morning came, the CD arrived in the mail. I know I am again exposing my naivety thinking such a small gesture of connection may have had an impact so great that my achievements would dwarf all those of addiction support specialists who had failed before me, but, well, you never know. And I felt I had to try. I arrived at Steve's bungalow around lunchtime. It was a balmy summer's day, clear enough that from the front garden you could comfortably make out the majestic mountains on the other side of the border. The unfortunate thing about balmy summer days is that they make stale urine smell a fair bit worse than it normally does, and the bungalow smelt horrendous on this day.

I called out to Steve, who was sober, compos mentis, and lying in bed. I decided to use this opportunity to talk to him about his life, maybe tapping into some trauma that led to him taking the path he had. He asked for a glass of water. I went through to the kitchen. Except for the literally dozens of Jacob's Creek bottles in the recycling bin, the kitchen was spotless. The care agency was obviously committed to ensuring Steve's living space was well kept. There were a series of notes stuck to the fridge with magnets:

"Dad, stop drinking start living."

"Dad, love you always."

"Dad, call me if you need anything."

They were all signed with the name Ben, and a drawn smiley face.

Steve was realistic when we discussed his life. He disclosed that the notes were old, his son had since moved to London with work, and they rarely spoke:

"We haven't fallen out or anything, he just hates seeing me like this".

It transpired Steve had a few family members very close by, but gradually one by one, they had all grown weary with trying to love him and ceased contact.

For my information, I just needed to know why. Was there some trauma from childhood, an experience perhaps? There must have been something that pushed Steve into this way of life. What Steve told me contradicted everything I thought I knew about addiction: nothing.

Steve talked of an idyllic childhood. As a young adult, his band toured the world, played huge venues and sold a good amount of records; then he met a beautiful woman with whom he had two children. He had lived every dream and ambition he set for himself as a young man. His conclusion knocked me sideways. Steve just liked being drunk more than he liked being a husband, a father or a musician. He was understanding of the many friends and family members who no longer wanted to watch him drink himself into an early grave and bore them no grudge. He gave me nothing to work with, nothing to cling to, nothing to support him with.

Steve's glam rock band had started in Cardiff in the late 70's and was immersed in a culture of alcohol. Gradually, one by one, everybody left the party leaving Steve there on his own, and there he remained, stagnating, idle, lonely, but crucially, free from any self-pity. His band fired him when he became a liability, he sold his studio when it became too time consuming, and he drank the proceeds. His wife and children left soon after. Steve accepted this as his lot, his consequence. He had made his bed, and he was more than happy to lie in it, in every sense of the expression. Steve had nothing to blame his alcoholism on and freely admitted his life was a choice. My hope for him was fading fast.

Just as I was leaving, I pulled a Columbo style 'just one more thing' and gave Steve the CD I was so proud to have found. He thanked me politely and put it on his bedside table next to his mobile phone that never rang, and a months old copy of Mojo magazine. It was still there the last time I saw Steve several weeks later. That night the care agency called me to complain that Steve had made sexual advances to two female carers who were trying to clean faeces off him. I reflected on what I thought I knew about connection and swore this would not dampen my resolve.

The reality of working with addicts is their standards change, and generally decline, as their addiction progresses. The abnormal becomes the normal. I'm sure there would have been a time where Steve thought attempting to flirt with two women who were cleaning his own faeces off him may have been in some way inappropriate, or at least undignified, but he did not feel like this now. Upon having the discussion where I had to very delicately, but very assertively tell him that his sexual advances were not welcome from his carers, Steve apologised and said it wouldn't happen again.

As with many addicts, there was no happy ending with Steve. He would sporadically swear he wanted to get sober, but never last more than an hour or two. On the last such case, Steve had been visited during the night by a care agency doing a safety check. They had cleared all the wine bottles from by Steve's bed. By the time I visited with a colleague at one in the afternoon, he had consumed another seven bottles in around six hours. To this day I remain in the dark about how his finances supported such an excessive and habitual addiction.

We talked more about sobriety, recovery, call it what you will. But the reality was that Steve had chosen alcohol over his marriage, his children, his career and his wellbeing. He'd chosen alcohol over everything and was devoid of self-pity or regret. Recovery must come from within, no addict will stay sober without the will to remain so. To choose sobriety now, Steve would have to accept his loneliness and stagnation without alcohol to numb the fear and isolation. This was not a task he was willing to attempt.

Every social worker needs to understand this: even if you approach a case with an open mind and an open heart there is still a possibility (a probability when working with addicts) that there will be no positive outcome, no happy ending. But what I intrinsically learned was this- it's not about outcomes, we are supporting people who have free will and who don't always have their own best interests at heart. The only question that matters when our day at work finishes should be:

"Have I done everything I can possibly do to help this person today?"

If the answer is yes, you should be able to walk away from work with a clear conscience and ready to go again the following day, with an open mind and an open heart.

I left the service shortly after this. The last time I saw Steve he was face down after a fall from bed, with an incontinence pad that I had placed between the floor and his groin so he could urinate without getting any on the carpet. He was slurring his words, swearing and making derogatory comments about me and whichever another person popped into his mind. I called the ambulance, waited with him until it arrived, and let the ambulance crew (who were already on first name terms with Steve) into the bungalow. Steve had made his choices. I didn't like them, but they were his own. He didn't want my help, and he certainly didn't want to be sober. I left with my enthusiasm undented. I knew I would never see him again. A few weeks later one of his ex-bandmates shared on social media that he had died. His short tribute harvested two likes and one share.

Supporting addicts can be one of the most frustrating, challenging, gut wrenching and thankless tasks we can do with our time, whether as a loved one or as a professional. As discussed, the abnormal becomes the normal, and standards continue to drop to enable us to get a fix of whatever it is we are addicted to.

Recovery must come from within. At some point your life must become so beyond control, so painful, so undignified that you simply no longer accept your predicament. For me, that moment was a Friday night out where I was kicked out of a pub and ended up squaring up to two nightclub bouncers in town. I later reflected with horror how life would have looked had a colleague, a friend, a client, or a patient have seen me that night, or how a conviction for drunk and disorderly might be explained to HR when my criminal record check needed renewing. That was my bottom, my enlightenment, my realisation that change was needed. More of this later.

I could never figure out why Steve, through all of his incontinence, falls, abandonment, indignities, failures, and eventual disability, never ever thought to himself that he was as low as he could go, and that change was needed. But I had to accept it. It was his battle to fight and for whatever reason he didn't feel like fighting. Maybe he didn't see the self-worth in himself that I saw in him. Maybe I was naïve to think I could save him, or change him, or at least enable him to change himself.

Addiction is hard to empathise with unless you've been there or at least witnessed it first-hand. It seems so curable, but telling an alcoholic to stop drinking is as futile as telling somebody who is Anorexic to just form healthy eating habits. The key to good social work is ensuring that when you find somebody you can help, you're not grizzled by negativity and cynicism from trying to help those you can't. There are people out there who you can help, and who you can make a difference to. It's just about controlling the controllable and understanding that some people do not want to change. We must accept this and move on. If we can honestly say we have done everything we can to help that person, we can finish our day with a clear conscience.

I'm not sure Steve ever opened up to me fully. I can't honestly believe that a man with no adverse childhood experiences, no notable experiences of trauma, who had lived a fruitful, creative and happy life would honestly let all of that go simply because he liked being drunk. Maybe I just got to him too late, but on the other hand there was plenty of evidence of people reaching out to support him to get sober unsuccessfully. The thing I got desperately wrong is that Steve crosses my mind constantly, he's the anomaly, the exception. Sometimes you have to accept, not that somebody is beyond help, but that they do not want your help.

I can't name a single person (known to me, or famous) who was coerced into getting sober who managed to stay that way against their will. You can have the most support, guidance, love and anything else you might need, but if the person isn't willing to recover and prioritise recovery, then there is nothing to work with and zero chance of success.

The difficulty is that addiction creeps slowly into your system, navigates its way into your psyche and burrows itself into your conscience and cognition. Nobody smokes, drinks or injects just the one time then becomes an addict overnight. I often imagined Steve's journey through addiction. His first hangover, the first time he vomited, the first time he woke up feeling remorseful, the first time he got arrested, lost his driving licence, the first time he got shouted at by a ward sister for drinking alcoholic hand gel, the first time he realised his mobility was gone. I imagined it all and couldn't understand why he never decided that enough was enough. Like approximately 90% of alcoholics, Steve was never able to get sober. I reflected, soul-searched and adventured through every dark corner of my mind to try to understand why. Eventually, all I could offer myself was acceptance. This was who Steve was, alcohol was his crime, it was also his punishment. It was his problem and his solution. I had good intentions and a slither of connection, but this would never be enough to rid Steve of his demons. It was a literal drop in the ocean. It wasn't up to me to consider what he could have become, what he could have achieved. This was neither my place nor my responsibility. Nobody blamed me, but I could never come to terms with my role as just another professional who tried and failed to help.

Nobody's help would have done any good for Steve unless he wanted to help himself, and he didn't. The only consolation, stark as it was, was that Steve lived and ultimately died on his own terms. All the good intentions and CD's in the world wouldn't make a difference.

Chapter Three

Matthew

July 2020

Summer 2020. Nobody needs to be told how much the world had changed by 2020. I was firmly and very happily finding my way in palliative care at my local hospice. It was the type of social work I had trained for (more about helping people, much less about bureaucracy). It tapped far more effectively into my skill sets of creativity, communication and initiative rather than being process led with an abundance of middle managers trying to save the local authority money for no gain or advantage of their own, other than professional credibility. Whenever somebody asks what you do, and you reply 'social work' there is generally a variation of one of these three responses:

1. That must be really challenging.
2. That must be very rewarding.
3. I couldn't do that.

To which I reply to a variation of

1. "Yes, it is".
2. "Yes, it is".
3. (On a good day) "Well, it has its moments", or (on a bad day) "No you probably couldn't".

It was 18th May 2020. The relevance of this date would serve to live long in the memory for many families. Subsequently we would learn that those who governed us were having a party on this day. One senior MP, Michael Fabricant, then went on to defend this action stating it was no different to hospital staff having a drink together after a long shift. This never happened. There was no truth in the suggestion that this ever happened. The arrogance, ignorance, contemptibility and duplicity of that government will live long in my memory. It was the ultimate betrayal. I saw, daily, the sacrifices my colleagues made. I watched in awe as they cared for people with Covid, before vaccinations were introduced, without being fully in the knowledge of what they were dealing with or how much danger they were in. We spent time away from our families, from each other, we didn't see our children to keep them safe. I saw super-human sacrifices from my friends and colleagues.

So, Fuck You, Michael Fabricant. I hope with all sincerity that you get your hands bound together and you spend eternity with an itchy anus.

I am happy at any given time, on any given day, in any given company, to share at length and in the greatest of detail my disdain for the Conservative Party. This will never, ever change. and it will be a cold day in hell before my opinion alters. Digression over.

It was a beautiful day, warm, breezy, blue skies. I walked to work during most of this period, enjoying and anticipating the incoming summer, making the most of the deserted streets, appreciating the rare species of wildlife that became ever more visible and confident as the people and their vehicles succumbed to lockdown.

At the hospice, many administrative, support and non-clinical departments were either furloughed or sent to work from home. The inpatient unit was very different. As the social worker on duty, ward rounds went on as normal, but with PPE always worn by all staff.

Upon arrival at work, I would walk to the changing room next to the ward entrance, wash, change into scrubs, put on a mask which was to be worn for the duration of the shift when in the room with other people, and anti-bac my hands after touching any surface. This was a warm spell; any patient or family contact involved the wearing of aprons and rubber gloves also. My respect for my colleagues, nurses, doctors, support staff, health care assistants and catering could not have been higher.

The fear of Covid weighed heavily on us all. Special protocols were in place for supporting people who were Covid positive, which involved wearing enhanced and very restrictive head and face protection that all but destroyed any possibility of developing a normal patient/social worker relationship.

It was a surreal and frightening time, but the levels of commitment and professionalism that my colleagues showed was faultless. Sometimes a colleague would go off with Covid, uncertain of a time they would return to work. Shifts would constantly need covering but would be covered without fuss or the requirement of thanks. What kept me motivated during this time was that we were needed more than ever, and when you go to work with people who are prepared to risk their lives to care for others (as far as we were concerned at the time), you don't feel fear, or a sense of entitlement. You feel privilege that you can work when others can't, either due to furlough, redundancy or poor health, and pride that every one of your colleagues on the frontline is getting on with their day selflessly and fearlessly for the good of their patients and their families.

18th May 2020 was a usual Covid day. I walked up the road to work along deserted paths, through the sun-soaked and leafy grounds of the council offices and to the Hospice. I made my way to the ward for the routine morning handover.

Sometimes you arrive on the ward and, well, you just know something a bit different is happening, or to put it realistically, something a bit worse than normal.

The ward manager asked to see me and explained the situation: there was a young woman receiving end of life care on the ward. I asked the usual questions about disease and prognosis but was met with a pause. Not the kind of pause where you don't know what to say, but the kind of pause where you just don't want to say it. The ward manager explained to me that this was a young lady (early 40's) who had attempted suicide by painkiller overdose. She had taken seemingly enough medication to end her life and left her husband Matthew a note. He continued to tell me that she had caused herself significant harm, enough to kill her but not instantly, and so here she was in the ward. At times like this the sense of jeopardy is palpable. There are many spoken interventions considered, the polite and professional 'so what do you need from me?', the slightly more abrupt, 'ok, what do you want me to do about it', or the good old fashioned 'just get to the fucking point, yeah?'. To sum up, as Matthew's wife had attempted to end her life, the police had become involved and taken the suicide note as evidence. Matthew had never read the note. He couldn't bring himself to. And now… now they needed somebody to sit in the sun house by the carpark (no other rooms were usable in Covid time), put on full PPE (mask, gloves, apron) and read Matthew's wife's suicide note to him.

Reflecting upon this day, it is one of those occasions whereby you just say 'yes' and do it. To consider the enormity of it, to empathise, to pay due consideration to how we might present the words, the responsibility becomes too great. It's too big a cross to bear so auto pilot takes over and away we go.

"Which room is he in?"

"7"

"Is it ok to go in now?"

"Yes"

"OK, I'll do it now".

"Are you ok?"

"Yes".

Room 7 was a mercifully short walk from the doctor's office. The crunching and crumpling of plastic as I applied gloves, mask and an apron proved a more cumbersome task than normal. I looked through the window. Matthew was there, sitting at his wife's bed. She was asleep, evidently at peace from whatever shattering motivation had brought her here. I knocked on the door. Matthew looked up and beckoned me in. He was a short, slightly built man with piercing blue eyes and dark hair. His clothes were casual but clearly expensive (trainers, leather jacket, designer brand shirt, black jeans).

"Matthew?"

"Yes."

"Andrew."

"Hi. Thank you for doing this."

"You're welcome." I indicated towards the patio doors in his wife's room.

"Shall we?"

We had about 90 seconds to walk from the main hospice building, round the large pond and up a brick pathway to the summerhouse. I made small talk. The weather, the journey in, just small talk. If there had been a handbook called "what to say to a man before you read his wife's suicide note to him", I would have read and referred to it, but let's be real here, the market for a book like would be niche verging on sluggish, so I was very much on my own with this one. The weather and the journey in would have to do. We sat together in the summer house. The garden chairs at 45 degrees from each other, with a feint smell of creosote and cobwebs. We sat briefly in silence.

"Shall I just read it verbatim?"

"Please".

The letter was a hurt, angry, sad, broken, sorry and apologetic reflection. Matthew's wife had drunk wine whilst writing it, taking pills, and crying as she did so. The more she drank and ingested, the more scrawling and illegible her handwriting became. She talked of their sex life, and her disappointment in it, her lament that they hadn't had children, her own perceived failures after getting a first-class degree from Edinburgh University but never going above entry level in a job. There was anger, hurt and vitriol all cushioned by me, trying to do what I could to take the rapier edge off the heartbreak by reading aloud softly.

When we had finished, I handed Matthew the letter. He took it silently and put it in his jacket pocket. We left the summer house in silence, and I walked him back to his wife's room where she lay peacefully, unconscious, and completely unaware of the crucifying impact of her words. I left Matthew alone and walked slowly back to the office. Nodding to the many who asked me if I was ok.

The truth is that I was ok. I knew what had happened, I was aware of the enormity of it, I was also aware that I was falling short on empathy. I had no point of reference to empathise with Matthew. The slow death of a loved one, the vitriolic note, the fact that the loved one had chosen suicide. I hoped it was filtering into my conscience and the response would come later, rather than me suffering from a debilitating stall in my empathy. The enormity was too much. It was like losing your temper over misplacing a twenty-pound note but feeling nothing if you lost a million. The enormity, the impact, the connection with Matthew. It was overwhelming. I found subsequent supervisions didn't cover my feelings on the matter either, just that I knew it had happened but didn't really feel a great deal.

I've since found this is a common occurrence in palliative care work. We are so immersed in death, displays of emotion, love, that we can't always react wholeheartedly to every occurrence, every death, every conversation. Imagine you're pushing a boulder up the hill to a cliff, it takes shunts, and shoves and pushes and heaves. Eventually you get the boulder to the edge of the cliff. The tiniest push is enough to get the boulder over the edge. Our emotional responses aren't always responses to one thing and one thing alone; often they are an aggregate response to a number of things that have happened. Maybe my connection with Matthew was something that pushed me 90% of the way but wasn't the crucial final push that shoved me over the edge.

It is also possible that I couldn't find time to prioritise myself when I was so worried about Matthew, which I did. He was the client that comes along every now and again that keeps you awake at night. You dread the phone call saying he has died by or attempted suicide, or gone missing, or been taken somewhere for his own protection. But Matthew held it together pretty well. His wife died 7 days after we first spoke. When I called him the day after, he was realistic, almost relieved. He had taken the few days since the suicide attempt to take stock and process what had happened. He had accepted his wife's decision and although he wasn't comfortable with her reasons, he acknowledged the end to her suffering and by default, the beginning of his own. Matthew was disarmingly frank when we spoke on the phone.

"She'd been ill for a long time. Mentally ill. I mean, her health, her mental health, it wasn't good". Matthew was a kind, gentle and articulate man with a background in construction work. He was aware of his language and ensuring he said the right words:

"If I ever offend anyone I don't mean to, it's just where I'm from." Matthew explained, with absolutely no need whatsoever. Matthew spoke, as many relatives of the tormented and traumatised do, of his relief that she was now at peace.

"Sometimes when she wasn't in a good place, she would go for a walk alone to clear her head."

"I dreaded the phone call, saying she'd be found, or arrested, or was dead, or they wanted me to identify the body. And now…." I gave Matthew time. No interruption was needed.

"Last week, I finally got the call saying she was gone. That she was dead. I was relieved. She was out of pain, out of harm's way. I was relieved. Is that awful?".

"*No*" I replied compassionately, but in a very knee jerk, automatic way that suggested I had gone for the easy answer rather than the correct one.

"You love her. You knew she was in pain. Now she's died the only one suffering is you, and because you love her unconditionally, you're relieved. Your response is a beautiful one and one that just evidence what I didn't need proved, that you loved her unconditionally. You're not paying any attention to your own pain, just hers. That's what you do when you love somebody".

My panicked mind had struck gold. Matthew was happy with my response, as much as I was surprised by it. We talked about imminent plans. Matthew talked about the funeral, cremation, the admin, the registration of death, how many copies of the certificate to get and what he was going to do with his wife's clothes and possessions.

"I want to go on holiday, is it ok if I go on holiday?" Matthew asked, like he was asking his teacher if he could go to the toilet.

"You don't need my approval for anything Matthew," I sensed this was why he was asking me.

"Where are you going to go?".

"Cornwall, near the Minack Theatre, South Coast. Steph loved it there." This was the first time he had used his wife's name.

"We'd go down there camping, then on the last night we'd always go to the Minack and see whatever was on; Shakespeare, Musical, Gilbert and Sullivan, whatever. The theatre is carved out in the rock of the cliff. All you can see is the stage and sea, nothing else. After the show I'd ask Steph if she enjoyed it, but I know really, she was just lost staring at the sea, ships on the horizon, the sunset. She was content. I never wanted more than for her to be content". There was silence over the line.

"Shall we talk again next week?"

"Yes please" whispered Matthew, stifling sniffs, and I suspect tears.

"I'd appreciate that very much".

We agreed a time and I completed a referral for Matthew to be put on my caseload. I advised Matthew (much against Hospice guidelines) that I would be his allocated worker for as long as he needed me to be. I correctly suspected our work had only just begun.

Chapter Four

Greg

May 2018

'You cannot reason someone out of something he or she was not reasoned into' (Jonathan Swift).

There can be an overwhelming mix of emotions when supporting somebody in palliative care. Sometimes you meet somebody you bond with, sometimes the opposite. Sometimes you meet people who are inspiring, funny, courageous, reflective, miserable, bitter, resentful - the list is long. And then sometimes you meet people who can just make you laugh.

I can remember one occasion being asked to visit a patient who, like many others, had gone through life procrastinating about getting his affairs in order. He had no last will and testament (although very little to leave), no partner, a family that was estranged (we never quite got to discussing why, but he said he understood), but most critically no funeral plans. A quick chat and a google search led me to a local provider who sent out a form to fill in with some specifications around music, readings and the like. There is a skill to a pre-very-important-and-potentially-distressing-chat. It's important to segue at the right point. Greg was a local man in his early 50's. For one who was without people who cared about him, he was incredibly likeable, and oddly he looked well. This is one of the things that can really throw you in palliative care. A person can seem so well one day, then things just change and suddenly they are asleep and unlikely to wake up.

Greg seemed well, his face full of colour, a full head of dark greying hair, in fact, were I not visiting him in the context I was, I would struggle to believe he was even unwell. But there we were, discussing how he wanted his funeral to go. Greg was chatty and fearless. It never ceases to amaze me how many people move towards end-of-life care with good grace and serenity, often reflectively, sometimes with an element of anxiety or regret, but Greg seemed grateful for the life he had had and perceived his forthcoming young death as a means to an end for his excesses; he had drunk and smoked heavily for the vast majority of his adult life.

"How are you doing?"

"Morning And, well I ain't buying any green bananas boss, put it that way" he responded in a rustic, part Herefordshire part Gloucestershire rustic brogue.

"You ready to talk funerals?"

"Well, unless Susan Boyle rocks up". I genuinely have no idea what he meant by this, or even if he meant Susan Boyle.

"I'll take that as a yes".

"Take it any way you like Butty. Fire away".

"Right. Music. What music do you want at the funeral?"

"I don't care".

"What do you mean you don't care?"

"Well, I'll be dead, won't I?"

Patients receiving hospice care aren't usually quite so pragmatic and direct, but I could see where this was going.

"OK", I replied moving gingerly on:

"How about flowers?"

"Nah. No flowers".

"Why not?"

"I've got hay fever".

At this point our discussion moved from, what I hoped would be a compassionate, humane and professional discussion into a playful bicker about his absence of logic. What's notable here is that Greg was in a shared room, and he was indifferent towards the patient and family in the bed opposite hearing the conversation. I was wary of the potential issues this might cause but was keen to pursue the 'therapeutic' (and I use inverted commas on purpose here) relationship I had already developed in short time.

This is one of the fundamentals about palliative care, often, it doesn't take the shape we thought it would. Our expectations are nearly always in some way incorrect. Families we expect to cause issues can be delightful, a seemingly straight forward piece of work can reveal a maelstrom of safeguarding concerns, and a quick conversation can turn into hours. Often the story told by case notes or support plans is not the full story. The nuances of humanity present in all their complexities in palliative care. People with a reputation for being surly or obstreperous can prove charming and funny, people who have dedicated their lives to helping others and giving of themselves may choose to spend their final days in isolation, much to the distress of family members and loved ones. I am recalling a lady who was being supported with her end-of-life care saying a passionate, heartfelt and structured goodbye to her husband. I'm uncertain of the full text, but I know they spoke of their mutual love, how grateful they were to have found each other and to have lived so happily together. They embraced, they kissed, they said goodbye. And then… she didn't die. She lived on for another week. She made the decision that, having said her goodbyes, it would be too painful to see her husband again. He was devastated but understanding. She was, to use his words, "a stubborn old bugger who knows her own mind". Empathy is at the forefront of any therapeutic relationship. Quite how you empathise with a man whose wife is at the end of her life but doesn't want to see you I am uncertain, but never forget tea and sympathy.

Greg and I continued our conversation in the same fashion, having conversations more appropriate for a pool hall or Sunday league changing room. My intervention was short, but the longer we talked I noticed that Greg, as funny and sharp as he was, was totally incapable of sincerity or serious conversation. The man was a mystery and clearly wanted to remain so. I visited Greg a total of three times, his funeral was planned with great simplicity and various offers of support for him, or his estranged family were declined. On my third and final visit, our conversation went as before, a bit about football, a quick and sweary critique of British politics, followed by a detailed and elongated debate around which of the two major hamburger chains provided superior junk food. I was just signposting towards the end of the session (this usually consisted of a quick look at my watch, followed by slapping hands on my knees then proclaiming 'right then'), when Greg interrupted me.

"Mate, can I ask one favour?" He sounded forlorn, like he hadn't sounded before in my company.

"I need to write a letter. To my little girl. Well, she's 23, she hasn't spoken to me for a while but I just… can you write it down for me?"

I got the distinct impression from Greg that he'd been working up to this, maybe he was working out if he trusted me, maybe he was just working out in his own mind what he wanted to do. Greg didn't seem like he opened-up often, so I felt the need to ensure I empowered him to make the most of his openness. I pulled out the pad and pen that sat permanently and uncomfortably in my back pocket.

"It's to my daughter" he began "so, Dearest Jess" to start with, I think.

"Jess" Greg said again, it was as though just saying her name unleashed remorse in him. He was choked and suddenly trying with all his strength not to cry.

"Jess" Greg repeated. "I wanted you to know that the day you were born was the greatest day of my life. You were conceived and born in love and although I have been an absolute failure as a father, my intentions were good. I loved your mum with all my heart and doing what I did ruined everything for me, you and her. I regret everything that has happened in my life. Your mum didn't deserve it, and you certainly didn't".

Greg took a breath. The floodgates were open, I wasn't sure how long he'd been bottling this up or if he'd ever apologised or acknowledged wrongdoing before, but here he was, and here I was. I was intrigued but felt a huge weight of responsibility that I may be hearing first hand confessions. Steve composed himself, took two more deep breaths from his bed, rested his hands in his lap and continued:

"The day you were born was my proudest and happiest ever, I remember the midwife handing me to you and I just stared into your eyes. You were brand new, fresh, beautiful, helpless and just so perfect. I vowed there and then that no harm would ever come to you. Never in a million years did I think that the person who would hurt you the most would be me".

Greg sensed the discomfort that was clear in my face. What the hell had he done?

"Don't panic chap, I'm not a nonce". Greg had correctly anticipated my concerns and put my mind at rest for which I was relieved.

"Cracking!" I replied enthusiastically. *"Cheers for that."*

"I'll probably be able to focus a bit better now".

"You were ten months old when I left you and your mum. I want you to know, as you know there was somebody else and it didn't last, there was never a minute that went by that I didn't regret letting you down. The day me and Carrianne decided we wanted to be together, she had just left her bloke, and I was on my way home to tell your mum it was over between us, and I was leaving. Just before I got to the front door, I looked through the window. You were in a highchair and your mum was feeding you. I swear I never felt an intoxicating love for anybody or anything as I felt for you that moment. I hadn't even told your mum I was going, and I felt sick at the thought of it. Within twenty minutes I was gone, I had broken your mum's heart, left her without income and bills to pay and abandoned the one thing that was more precious to me than life itself: you."

"I just want you to know that I will soon be dead, not suicide, I'm in the hospice and my cancer is about to take me. I want nothing from you, just to know and understand that I love you, and that every day that I was away from you was a day wasted with remorse and regret, knowing I missed so many firsts, so many moments and memories. You may hate me but nowhere near as much as I hate myself. I will love you until my last sorry breath. This will be soon".

Greg lay back in his bed and turned away to face the window. His sobs were audible. He had gone in the shortest of moments from the funny man to the morose. Although he had wronged and ruined his family, all I could see in him was sorrow. I hoped that his daughter would receive the note and read his words as I had heard them, with sincerity and absolute apology.

Greg was able to write down Jess' address, which was only a short drive from the hospice. He cried uncontrollably for a while then fell asleep. I left him in peaceful, relieved exhaustion and took his letter to the post room.

Greg died peacefully four days later. None of his family members made contact.

Chapter Five

The Two Phils

July 2018

Phil was a lovely man who attended the men's patient social group I run at the hospice for many years. He had been a successful businessman for decades, success reflected in his car, his clothes, the articulate and graceful way he spoke and the beautiful country cottage he shared with his wife. Phil had never smoked but found himself with a diagnosis of lung cancer when he was thriving in every sense of the word at the age of 50. His diagnosis turned his life upside down, but he soon applied his business acumen and impressive motivation and spirit to our group, coming up with ideas for fundraising, awareness raising, and generally making the world around him a better place for everyone.

Phil had a best mate at the group, also called Phil. Phil and Phil grew from being blokes in a social group to good friends and eventually the rocks of the whole gang and ambassadors for it too. New members would be introduced and inducted by them, visitors to the hospice would be given elegantly crafted monologues into the importance of the group, but more than anything else, they would relentlessly take the piss out of each other and anybody else. On one occasion a lovely and wholly innocent volunteer horticulturist (and by 'innocent' I mean she didn't deserve to be emotionally tortured by a room full of terminally ill men) visited us. She was happily talking through some of the flowers and plants the chaps could grow at home.

"…and if everything goes well, you'll start to see buds in the next eight to ten months" she said.

"Well, that's no fucking use to us then is it" said Phil Two: "my missus won't even let me buy Duracell batteries". The poor, dear, lovely and wholly innocent volunteer horticulturist looked distraught as the guffaws rang out. She went a shade of puce, finished her presentation and never darkened our doorstep again. Phil One chatted to her at the end of the session explaining that this darkest of dark humour was the one thread that connected all of the men as they adopted unique approaches to considering their own, and very pending, mortality.

The Phil's double act garnered a reputation that led to everyone from senior members of management to community nursing, housekeeping, catering and everyone else just finding excuses to drop by and generally get the piss taken out of them. Local police officers were given requests to score cannabis (for medicinal reasons), one of the chaps asked if his mate could visit the group to demonstrate his hobby ("He's REALLY into controlled explosions"), and one chap was quite open and happy to give the full gory details of his armed robbery conviction ("we all make mistakes when we're young"). Through it all, Phils One and Two were the backbone, settling disputes, blagging free tickets for things and generally living each day like it was their last.

Phil One's disease progressed quickly and aggressively around about the time the Covid pandemic changed the way the UK lived forever. Our meetings went online, using Zoom to catch up once a week. This meant we gained members who were unable to come to physical meetings but could work their way around technology, but also meant we lost the chaps who feared the concept. Our group had managed a career best the previous of year of going 364 days without a death: an unheard of, almost 'perfect game' for the team. This lulled me into a false sense of security. I thought they were ill but not that ill. I thought it was a hoax: that this group, hosted by the hospice, attended by patients, was just a social group for blokes who were just a bit wheezy. Phil One was the first of eleven to go into end-of-life care in a 12-month period.

The signs were there: weight loss, a phone call from his community nurse saying his disease was starting to progress, he started to appear on screen for meetings with an oxygen mask on, until the inevitable phone call. Phil was coming into the inpatient unit. This could mean one of the two things, he was receiving symptom control so doctors could do a bit of trial and error with his medication to get him well enough to return home, or he was coming in to receive end of life care. As soon as I saw his name on the list, I went to the inpatient unit to see him. He was in a single room, sat up on his bed eating tuna pasta and, and this was very noticeable, looking very well.

Phil looked a little confused by my Covid mask and gown but soon recognised me. "Hello mate", he said in his smooth executive home counties accent. "Nice to see you".

"Hi mate" I replied, trying to smile in a comforting way but quickly realising I was wearing my Covid mask, *"I can come back when you've finished if you like"*.

"That'd be great" said Phil, "be nice to catch up, the internet coverage is shocking and there's no Sky or anything".

"No worries, mate" I chuckled, *"See you in 20 minutes".*

When I returned twenty minutes later, I discovered a different Phil. His usually elegant slicked back grey hair seemed ruffled and unkempt, his once confident body language was now slumped and beaten, and he was tearful. One of the great challenges of hospice work is trying to avoid asking stupid questions. 'Are you alright?' really isn't going to help a person who is the very definition of not alright. Ditto 'How are you?' I tend to favour open questions; it gives the person I am supporting flexibility and control over the conversation.

"Talk to me Phil" was my go-to on this occasion, and it worked.

"Nowhere is home. I'm in limbo. I don't belong anywhere. Wendy (his wife) has just left, she's going home. The home we've shared together for 25 years. I know every inch of that place and I'm never going back there. I'm staying here until I die. Which will be in the next few days most likely. This is the only home I will ever know for the rest of my life. This is limbo."

I sat lost. In silence. I looked at Phil and sat in the seat by his bed. There was nothing I could say, no consolation, no humour, no solution. All I could do was listen as he poured out in front of me. He reflected on a life led well, with buoyant finances, every holiday imaginable, rock climbing, running marathons, a hugely successful career in business. He did tell me what it was he did, but it never quite made sense. It was something to do with selling businesses to other businesses or something. Now, he was contemplating something he found impossible, a loss of control. Suddenly the outcomes of his life were no longer in his grasp, and with that slipping away, his sense of home, of belonging and even of existence were going with it. As a comparatively young patient his life was coming to an end. He talked and cried. I sat and listened. It was all I could do. We were beyond the age-old counselling skills of paraphrasing, summarising and reflecting. Phil needed to talk, and I needed to listen.

He sounded angry for the first time. A man who had never smoked having lung cancer dying before he turned 60, he and his wife had decided not to have children, so he had fewer visitors than most people in his situation. He'd spent a long time obsessing over work and not taking time out to enjoy what he had. He was reflecting on, and seemingly angry about every decision he had ever made. Eventually Phil burned himself out. His conversation turned to how lucky he was to have found his wife, a complete soulmate, how much he appreciated our group and the fact I had run it for so long, and how, despite everything he had said, he was happy with life and comfortable that, although it wasn't at the time of his choosing, he had lived happily and well. The first time I looked at the clock we had been talking for two hours. Phil was sleepy so we shook hands, thanked each other for the time we had spent together, and vowed to speak again soon.

"Give the lads my best, won't you? Tell them where I am and what's going on" Phil called as I awkwardly removed my mask and gown at the door.

"Will do, take care Phil".

The group was meeting online the following day. At the morning handover meeting we were told that Phil had had an agitated night, was now asleep, but was certainly actively dying. I knew it was coming but the words 'actively dying' made my stomach churn. I'd heard them before. I'd heard them dozens of times, but this was different, this was real, this was Phil.

I dreaded the men's group session that day. This wasn't the first time the group had to be told about one of their number dying, but this was certainly the first time that information had been given online. There would normally be some quiet, some tributes, some time for consideration of the families, then maybe some light piss-taking and telling of funny stories. That was how they did it in person, but again this was different, this was online, impersonal and surreal.

I was acutely aware that Phil Two would be more aware of the situation than anyone else, they were in regular contact on WhatsApp and their respective diagnoses meant they was never any beating about the bush when it came to sharing the gory details. I started the meeting on Zoom and gradually saw the screen fill up with faces. Three appeared first and then Phil Two. He was a dry witted man, self-effacing and clever. He was a master of cracking the first joke after hearing of a group member's death and managing to get a laugh out of everyone, not today. He looked ashen, dark around the eyes and his usual never-say-die lust for life seemed to have left him in the cold on this coldest of days. I opened the meeting from the warmth of my lounge:

"Lads, there's no easy way to say this, Phil sends his best to you but he's at the hospice. He's there for end-of-life care".

The group talked for a while, serenely and with unusual compassion, evidently very aware of Phil Two's presence and his clear distress at the predicament of his friend. I asked at this point if the chaps wanted to record messages via my phone that I could play to Phil One so he could hear his friends wish him well one more time before he died. Some of the older lads had clearly misunderstood the assignment and shouted, 'get well soon' and 'hopefully see you next week' with thumbs aloft and the eternal hope of youth. Then it was Phil Two's turn.

"Hello mate. I just wanted to wish you luck on your journey. However, it happens, and wherever you go, good luck my friend. Go well. Love You, mate. Thank you for everything".

I sat and stared at the screen. I could see tears filling my own eyes and the other men in the group, moved by the resident joker's moment of absolute love, sorrow and sincerity. I had to dig deep to find a response.

"Thankyou Phil. That was beautiful" was as good as I could muster. The men continued leaving short, good luck

messages "I don't know you well, but I like what I've seen", "good luck mate, see you on the other side" and the like.

As the session closed, I promised the men I would drive straight to the hospice to see Phil and play him the messages. I'm not a spiritual person, but I was overwhelmed by a feeling of urgency, as if time was short and I needed to hurry.

I left quickly and got in my car and drove the short distance to the hospice. I was numb to it all. I knew it was sad, I knew it was incredibly emotive, but I just felt a little bit 'business as usual' about the whole thing. I shall highlight from personal experience the dangers of feeling like this later on.

The drive is short, less than ten minutes. I floated across the car park, swiped in and made the short walk into the inpatient unit. I found the ward sister:

"How's Phil doing?".

"I'm sorry, he died about 20 minutes ago".

"Is anybody with him?"

"No. His wife knows but she said her goodbyes last night and chose not to come in".

I thought for a moment. I'd promised his friends, and I'd promised Phil Two, so this was it.

"Can I see him?".

"Of course. Do you know which room he's in?"

I walked down to Phil's room. I was numb, my stomach was in knots. Personal conflict stirred within. I could just leave now if I wanted, forget the whole thing. I stopped. Dithered. Looked at my phone, then dressed in the face mask and disposable gown.

I knocked on the door. I knew I wouldn't get a response, but it seemed the right thing to do; good manners, dignity, compassion, I'm not sure, but I knocked the door gently and walked in. A privacy curtain covered the entrance to the room. I could see the light coming through the patio window of Phil's room. I pulled it across slowly and saw him. With the sun filtering through the gap in the curtains he was a mere silhouette from a few feet away. I walked up to the bed as I had done several times before and sat on the plastic chair. Phil's mouth was wide open, his drying and purple lips were motionless. His closed eyes seemingly gazing into the top of his head and his slicked back hair immaculate. He looked like his final act was to call out or gasp for breath, then nothing. Death.

I wasn't scared, freaked out, reflective, overwhelmed. In fact, I was none of the things I thought I would be. I was functional. I'd come with a job I promised I'd do, so I was going to do it. I sat with Phil and talked to him. I told him I was grateful for his support and his friendship and wished him a good rest. Then I took my phone out, found Phil Two's message and pressed play. For whatever reason it seemed no less moving, no less relevant to play it to him after he had died. It was Phil Two's goodbye and it deserved to be played, even if it wasn't heard. I played the other messages too, then played Phil Two's again:

"Hello mate. I just wanted to wish you luck on your journey. However it happens, and wherever you go on your journey, good luck my friend. Go well. Love you mate. Thank you for everything".

I put my phone into my pocket and sat a while longer, looking at Phil. I expected him to look just like he was asleep, but it was nothing like that. His skin was now ashen, his expression not something I'd seen on his face before, and the overwhelming stillness and silence of him was consolatory. Despite his pained expression, he was at peace. Peace radiated from him. His suffering was over. He had tolerated his last dose of chemotherapy, pressed his final call bell and cried his final tear.

I stood up, said goodbye, pressed my hand on his hand as it cooled and seized. Then I left. I walked up the seemingly endless corridor of the inpatient unit and walked past the ward sister:

"Are you alright?" she asked with genuine compassion.

"I am" I smiled; I hope warmly. I said, *"Thank you"* and walked on to get on with the rest of my day.

Chapter Six

Tony

November 2019

As discussed, some people you meet are inspiring, likeable, funny, interesting. Tony wasn't. I didn't like Tony, I hated him. That's nothing a professional social worker should say out loud. We should always find appropriate channels for our disdain, but in this case, I will make the exception, the reasons for this will become clear.

Whilst working in our day hospice service, I was asked my opinion on the complex case of an outpatient, a man with a fast-progressing form of motor neurone disease. There had been reports from his adult son of a text message saying that his partner was abusing him. There had also been a suggestion that his partner, a lady of a similar age, late 60's, had coerced him into marriage in recent weeks. The inevitable speculations about money grabbing were also present from those who knew the case. Tony was a respected member of his local community, a nearby well to do market town with an appetite for high culture, something Tony revelled in, volunteering at the local theatre and giving time to several arts committees. His Motor Neurone Disease had quickly robbed him of his ability to walk and complete most tasks for himself. In the weeks that followed it would also deprive him of his ability to communicate verbally.

As requested, I went to meet the patient in day hospice, but then recognised quickly that this was a multi-disciplinary safeguarding meeting that the patient was not present at. The first thing up for discussion involved the patient's two adult sons. They had requested a meeting with their father about why he had sent a coded text message saying he was at risk. The very fact that family members had their own safeguarding code was a red flag. I advised that no, the hospice was not a place to settle family disputes of any kind, and perhaps more appropriate would be to have a discussion with the patient away from any of his family members. The two sons had turned up to the hospice despite this. I agreed to speak to the two sons away from their dad to gain some understanding of what the issues were. I like to think as a social worker with a range of unusual and challenging experiences, that I am difficult to shock or catch off guard, but these revelations were hugely difficult to hear.

Tony had been estranged from his sons for a decade since he had been jailed for several years, having been found guilty of being a prolific and committed sex offender. He had abused children in his care over a long period when he lived in the North of England working as a social worker.

This was the first hurdle for me. He had worked as a social worker. He had sexually abused children in his care whilst working *as a social worker*. I was shocked by how much this affected me, by how angry it made and how, and this is a word I am reluctant to use in 2024, it offended me. Carl Rogers taught us about the importance of unconditional positive regard being at the forefront of any therapeutic relationship, and yet I *hated* this man. Not just his offending, not just for the young lives that were forever scarred by his sick lust, not just for the blight his actions had had on the job that I am passionate about. *Him.* I hated him, for all that he was, and all who he was, *I hated him.*

Ethically this was a minefield, as tolerant and understanding as my senior management had been, I didn't feel comfortable refusing my services to an individual on this basis. I had to find a way of establishing some unconditional positive regard, or, at the very least, find something in me that could replicate unconditional positive regard. In the same way a sex worker would have to facilitate the demands of a repulsive client without vomiting on them, I had to find a way to show compassion to a person for whom I had none and had no wish to have any. The following weeks were a haze of phone calls, emails, conflict, Tony changing his will to suit the requests of whoever was visiting him that day to placate and keep the peace and so on. Eventually Tony was admitted into the inpatient unit for symptom control. This was most likely because of the many safeguarding concerns that had been raised (wife against sons, sons against wife).

To summarise, these are a few of the things that happened while Tony was with us: He changed his will three times, two members of staff broke down in tears in supervision with me at different points, appalled by his crimes but challenged by an internal conflict to treat this man with respect and care; and, staggeringly his sons made up flyers with his wife's photo on, demanding she not be allowed into the hospice, and asked our volunteer receptionist to put them up and distribute them. I had various phone calls from the sons and Tony's wife. There were accusations of manipulation, lies, abuse and screengrabs of his wife's Google searches asking how quickly she could access Tony's money after he was dead were all evidenced. It was a messy, chaotic and wholly unpleasant time. Often where there is conflict, we can see both sides and think one side is in the right, or at least more in the right than the other. I must admit I wouldn't have been comfortable taking either side in this battle for the estate.

My mind changed after spending some time with Tony. At one point I saw him having a conversation with his son. By this stage he was communicating exclusively with a keyboard voice-box using one finger. His son asked him to pass on to his wife that they were keen to sort out visiting arrangements and the like and wanted to cease hostilities with her. He said he agreed, and he would talk to her. I subsequently saw him meet his wife an hour later where he denied having seen them and proceeded, if anything, to stoke up more division. He told her they had made more allegations; they were going to go to her house to take some possessions of his, and that they were trying to arrange a restraining order to stop her from visiting the hospice. It soon started to make far greater sense to me. Tony didn't just manipulate, gaslight and exploit those he was jailed for abusing. That was how he dealt with everyone close to him. The mess around his ever-changing will, the internal and ongoing accusations, it all came from Tony. To the outsider he was a timid, non-verbal palliative care patient, worthy of pity and sympathy. But I had got to know the real Tony. He was a manipulator, a liar and an abuser.

In all my time as a social worker I'd never met an individual who challenged my value set like Tony did. News of his death was met with indifference by those who knew his secret, but something I found hard to process and ignore, was that very few people knew the truth. The local press printed a glowing tribute of his contribution to a local arts centre. They talked of his innovation and creativity, how he gave so willingly of his time as an accountant to support local causes. Often when an individual is angry at somebody, we investigate why they are angry, and moreover, what benefit could come from letting them know how angry we are. I found my base responses to Tony challenging. I didn't like the emotions he provoked in me. I certainly didn't like his wife and rarely found a human as loathsome. I found the local tributes irksome; I would have taken great enjoyment and relief from adding a comment on the online newspaper that so glowingly and fondly remembered him, telling those who admired him how he was an offender of the most pitiful kind, how his sexual appetite had ruined lives; lives that continued, lives that would not be any the better for learning of his death. Or, in a base reflection of my basest of feelings I could've just written 'NONCE'. On reflection, I am pleased to disclose I did none of these. I closed the internet down and walked away with both mine and Tony's reputation intact.

When I think back, I can understand my reaction and how I felt about everything. I can remember supporting one of the nursing team who was just overwhelmed at the concept of supporting a child abuser. It threw up ethical questions about whether, in my eyes, every person was entitled to a 'good' death. In the cold light of the day, they are, of course they are. However, at that point, where our emotions are bubbling up to the service, our judgment is skewed, our concentration is disturbed, our sleep is poor, and we must dig deep to make an informed and objective judgment on how to work. Retrospectively, would I ever have gone online and told the world about what Tony did? No, of course not. However, there may well have been a time when I might have done. It's easy to disappear into the realms of fantasy here, to take a moment to consider how easy it would be, when he was at his most helpless, alone with me in his hospice bed, for me to share my final thoughts with him, to tell him what I really thought.

Over the years there have been countless periods where my patience and good nature have been tested to their very limits. I remember once supporting a young man who berated me constantly, criticised my speech as lazy, and spent many hours going on the internet bickering with people he wouldn't dare even look in the eye should he encounter them in real life. Did I point this out to him? No. This is one of the points where effective supervision is critical. The people we support can say hurtful things, sometimes picking at the personal feature we most dislike about ourselves and highlighting it to the world. Sometimes they will be critical of our working practices, sometimes fairly, yet sometimes unfairly (I genuinely don't know which one is worse).

The foot stamping, yelling, swearing, mimicking, offloading, ranting and temper losing needs to be bottled up, put away and taken into the office for supervision or a private moment with a colleague. This is a skill. Tony and his family stretched my good nature to the absolute limit. The advantage of this, is that when we've done it once, we know we can do it again.

I am happy to concede I got this wrong. I was hugely affected by his wife who wrote an incomprehensibly critical letter of complaint about me. This led to me yelling at a senior manager, paraphrasing Ricky Gervais, that the last time I'd read something that insane it was written on a wall in human shit. It wasn't my most professional moment, but it was certainly one of my most sincere.

When the inevitable post death court cases happened, I pleaded with our Caldicott Guardian to allow me to be the one that went to court to give evidence. This was obviously deemed inappropriate due to my lack of medical background. I had not managed my feelings effectively, meaning that although Tony was dead, he and his family were existing in my psyche, conflicting, bickering and slanging at each other. Consequently, here I am five years later angrily banging away on a laptop keyboard for my catharsis. I held on to Tony for far too long because I didn't talk about it at the time. If ever there was a good advert for supervision and talking about our feelings, this was it.

I've moved on from Tony. I hope his victims have found peace. I hope his sons and wife have found some closure, both with his wrongs, the conflict Tony created and each other. I hope they found a way to be ok with each other and move forward with their lives.

I've worked hard to move on but I'm afraid that after all of this catharsis I still can't find it in my soul to wish Tony rest in peace. The reports of his court case in the local newspaper told of how he had been sexually abused as a child, a common theme in the lives and development of abusers. I am disturbingly intolerant to this. It explains his behaviour, but it doesn't excuse it. It angers me that he built a new life, moved on from his crimes, started a new career, made new friends and constructed a reputation for himself while his victims continued living with what he did. Logical, social work educated me doesn't believe in an eye for an eye. But there was nothing apologetic about Tony. In recovery we are taught that the best form of apology is a change of behaviour. In Tony, even at the end of his life, I saw manipulation, misuse of power and deliberate lying and misleading, all facets of the abuser.

He hadn't changed in my eyes. I fully accept there is something unresolved about Tony for me, maybe I have made the age-old mistake of thinking 'well if you think it's hard, think of the victims'. Maybe I just need an hour with my therapist to put him to bed. The one saving grace is learning. From an entirely professional perspective I allowed Tony to get into my brain and disrupt me. I can remember one doctor who was a fantastic man but with a propensity for sarcasm asking if I was getting emotional support. Thinking he was joking as he usually was, I unwisely laughed it off. On reflection, I bottled it up, sealed the lid and shook the bottle. I've been carefully unscrewing the bottle ever since.

Chapter Seven

The long-lasting impact of hospice work

I remember in my dim and distant youth working in the pubs and clubs of my hometown, and every boss, manager and landlord would tell you the same thing- 'this is not a job, this is a way of life'. The same is true for hospice work. It changes how you look at life, it changes your mindset. The reality is you probably won't be the same person again. This isn't necessarily a bad thing. You just need to lean into the discomfort of the changes your mind has taken. However, without the right level of support and supervision you might just crash, and when you do it won't be pretty. I know this first hand. It started with a booming heartbeat when I wasn't exerting myself (although my GP was confident 5 or 6 black coffees a day were sharing the blame with any other external factors).

Many men I speak with talk about their emotions like they are a surprise, almost as if the things that should affect us don't, but the smaller things have a disproportionately greater impact. As previously discussed, It's as if we are pushing a huge boulder up to a cliff. Some exertions push the boulder a few metres, some a couple of feet, and others just an inch or two. The aggregate impact of this is a boulder that's on the edge of the cliff. The confusion comes when it takes the tiniest swish of a little finger to push it to go over the edge. I've seen this with myself, and others in hospice care. The death of somebody you know well and care about seemingly has a limited impact, but something of seemingly less importance has a far greater emotional effect. We need to get in the habit of talking about what has happened and accessing therapeutic supervision, even if we think we're ok, you never know, psychologically speaking, what is boiling up under the surface.

For my own part, I ended up with what I can only describe as secondary post-traumatic stress. This was largely a result of constantly sweeping my emotions under the carpet, constantly assuring people I was fine, when, whilst I was, I was sleepwalking into not being so. Before I knew it, I succumbed to a prevailing sense of gloom and pointlessness. Whether I was at a gig, watching rugby, football or theatre, I had the internal monologue telling me that this was all temporary, in 100 years none of this would be here and most of us would be gone and forgotten. Fun times, eh?

The lesson here is that if you are going to undertake this kind of work, the first thing you need to do is ensure there is adequate supervision, a solid culture of emotional support for colleagues, and a team that will understand and support you when you need to say 'no'. I appreciate this is easier said than done, and I'm the worst person for getting this wrong, but ultimately, not looking after yourself properly is a first-class ticket to not completing your first year in palliative care.

My own method for management of my emotions was to drink whisky, lots and lots of whisky. This may have slowed down or diverted my emotions a little, but the thing with emotions is, unless you deal with them, they will find a way to bubble up to the surface, whether you use prescribed medication, alcohol, illicit drugs or whatever else that floats your boat.

Many books and commentators on sobriety will tell you that you reach rock bottom when you choose to stop digging, I chose to stop digging after narrowly avoiding getting arrested for squaring up to two nightclub bouncers in one of the less high-end parts of town. It's not what this book is about but if you like a good solid piss up anecdote then read on and enjoy.

I was a big drinker, I collected Scotch Whisky, drank a lot of it, had qualifications in it, and even had a sideline in doing tasting events. Retrospectively, and having learned much about alcoholism and addiction, I can see that much of this was a subtle but very manipulative way of building up barriers between me and sobriety. I am Scottish on my mum's side and Whisky was a huge part of family reunions, Christmases, birthdays etc. After my uncle (a connoisseur well known in his part of the highlands) died, his birthday would be remembered with whisky, which would be photographed and sent to his wife. My wife and I would regularly visit distilleries, sending her a photo telling her we were thinking of my uncle. In fact, when I first told my wife I was going to stop drinking she responded:

"Are you sure? Whisky is such a huge part of your identity".

It was April 2023. My wife and I were having dinner in a local restaurant and had a very enjoyable bottle of red wine. Rather than go home we decided to go to a local wine bar where we drank three more bottles of red. There were a lot of people dancing, cavorting, falling off stools and generally contributing to a thoroughly debauched scene. At this point a bouncer, a clear foot shorter than me obviously, approached me and announced I had had too much to drink and would be leaving the premises. Experience told me that you don't argue with bouncers, a bit like Police, judges, traffic wardens and teachers. You're not going to win so don't bother, you might as well try and kick water uphill.

I had a limited knowledge of understanding about being ejected from licenced premises, meaning I didn't know that when you got kicked out of one, the security staff would radio round all of them to ensure you couldn't get in anywhere. A number of other pubs were visited, none of whom were prepared to offer us refreshment and hospitality on the aforementioned grounds. We eventually found a bar in a dubious part of town that would let us in. The bouncer, very much in the image of Anthony Joshua, took twenty pounds from us but then announced that we were only allowed to drink soft drinks on the premises.

After an hour of sitting and talking with my wife, we were finally allowed to get a pint of Guinness. The bouncer seemed to take exception to this, my still very inebriated wife took exception, I took exception to him taking exception, he advised me of his intentions to remove me from the premises. I took umbrage at this and advised that I would be leaving the premises of my own accord and had no intention of returning. As I walked out of the premises the bouncer pushed me in the back. I went into the street and, as the bouncer went to slam the door, advised him that I was displeased by his attitude and continued to remonstrate. At this point a bouncer from the lap dancing club opposite called over to me that he didn't approve of my conduct and felt that my best option would be to leave the area.

At this point, I stood in the middle of the street, beckoning my hands in the direction of each establishment and shouting:

"Come on then You Cunts, I'll take the pair of you on. Do you want some?".

The rest of the evening remains unclear, but my wife and I returned home without further incident. The summary was, that I was now on a list of people who were no longer welcome guests in the city's licenced premises.

I spent the Saturday drinking whisky while my wife slept the night off. I reflected on how unfair it was, how we weren't badly behaved and didn't justify the behaviour. Then it occurred to me; any of my patients, children I support, clients or colleagues could have seen me that night. A professional reputation is hard to build and easy to lose, and I could have lost it with significant aplomb. I was able to reflect on my life, I was addicted to alcohol, my life had become unmanageable and for the first time, I was not accepting of my situation.

The one thing whisky would do was shut the voices up for a bit. Don't worry, I know what you're thinking, I don't mean actual voices, more the constant ongoing Inner Monologue Goblin that treats every day like a party when you finally get sober. The Inner Monologue Goblin brings up people you supported years ago who have died, it reminds you of your own mortality and that, one day in the not-so-distant future we will all be dead and most likely forgotten. When my mental health is at its most dogged, The Goblin is intensive, repetitive and will not relent. So, if you're going to do palliative care work and you're going to do it sober, you are going to need some strategies to keep that Goblin at bay.

Confidentiality restricts what we can tell our loved ones over the dinner table or in the car on the way home, so an outlet is needed. I am the living, walking cautionary tale of what happens when you don't look after yourself effectively. Supervisions became a nice chat and a catch up with my manager, neglecting to mention things that had happened in that week. I'm speculating here, but bottling up the things I had seen, the people I'd known to die, and the impending grief that I supported people with left me bereft, broken, and unable to enjoy anything. Anything I would normally enjoy would be accompanied by The Goblin reminding me of the non-permanent nature of existence of everything. As my therapist put it, you can't use broken thinking to fix broken thinking.

I can guarantee you're better off looking after yourself from day one than going at things all out then crashing and trying to rehabilitate. Part of my reason for writing this is to keep my tedious and repetitive Goblin restrained and quiet.

At time of writing, I am approaching 12 months of continuous sobriety, and my Goblin is loving it. I can't pour booze on him to shut him up. Citalopram keeps him a little more sedate but ultimately, he's always there, reminding me about existence and the temporary nature of everything. He's like the pub bore whose opinion nobody asked for, but he's here, he's real and for the love of God he won't shut up.

So, look after yourself, because an Internal Monologue Goblin may well rear his head if you don't, and when he starts blethering it takes a lot of Citalopram and therapy to make him button his stupid Inner Monologue Goblin mouth. There, I said it. I've made mistakes so you don't have to.

What does looking after yourself look like? It means living and working healthily. A physically healthy lifestyle is a straightforward thing to attain, physical exercise, a healthy diet, if you smoke, don't smoke too much, if you drink, don't get too hammered. The usual, realistic targets one sets oneself when trying to attain a healthy lifestyle. Looking after yourself to attain good mental health is perhaps a little more challenging.

The first piece of advice I would offer would be that a problem shared is very honestly a problem halved. The more we talk about the things we have seen and experienced, the more our brain will allow us to process it healthily and, hopefully, sleep well and hopefully not invite any Inner Monologue Goblins into the fray.

We also need to learn how to say 'no'. This is never easy for anyone with a conscience. The very fact that we are being asked to do something means it is serious. If a case wasn't serious, it wouldn't be a matter for a hospice. If we overthink the consequence of everything we say 'no' to, we won't get much else done. As the old saying goes; 'you can't serve a drink from an empty vessel'. If we're empty, burned out, exhausted; we're no use to anyone. In supervision I was given some fine advice from my manager.

"If you never say 'no', what is your 'yes' worth?"

I have colleagues that swear by mindfulness, Yoga, religion, sport, running, climbing, and many other activities. Palliative care will take a place in your brain and set up camp there if you allow it to. If nothing else, a good wellbeing activity will provide distraction, it puts you right in the moment. Living in the moment is integral to healthy living. I know all of this because I didn't say 'no' for three years and ended up having an elongated and thoroughly intrusive period of poor mental health. The Inner Monologue Goblin got into my head, pitched a tent and a toilet block, and settled in for a long stay. By the time I realised who he was and what he was doing he was barbecuing sausages and on his fourth can of brown ale. My real concern at this point was he was going to pull out an acoustic guitar.

Here's how he works:

I watch sport.

Goblin: "None of this matters, in 100 years everyone here will be dead, and this will all be forgotten".

I go to a gig.

Goblin: "None of this matters, in 100 years everyone here will be dead and this will all be forgotten".

I have a lovely moment with my wife and daughter.

Goblin: "None of this matters, in 100 years everyone here will be dead and this will all be forgotten".

And so on, and so on.

It was at or around this point that it was time for therapy. I needed to shut the Goblin up. He was boring, repetitive and insisting on telling me things that I was already aware of to take the enjoyment out of any and every activity, Giving the Goblin an identity and a narrative was useful in therapy.

I spoke with a close and trusted female colleague of mine, a counsellor at work. I sought advice on sourcing therapy, counselling if you like, and wanted to know the pitfalls.

"Well first and foremost, you need to know about 75% of all counsellors are awful and shouldn't be in the job".

Now this was a revelation!

It gave me time to reflect on my time as a counselling student some twenty years previous. When I thought about it, I was the only person on the course who had never had counselling myself. One person, a father, had experienced unexplained cot death, his only child, he was in no place to help anyone and yet there he was. Another student was on so much lithium some of her teeth had been ground away and she was unable to hold a conversation. There were many people training who had failed to access counselling themselves and saw training as a kind of therapy or recovery for them. The same colleague who offered the stark evaluation of 75% of counsellors explained to me this was a well-established concept, known as *Training as the Preferred Treatment Modality.*

My colleague's advice was simple; research your therapist, speak to them, and ensure they have earned the right to hear your story. I found a therapist who only saw men, so assumed a level of speciality. Getting a therapist online is like ordering takeaway or choosing an Airbnb. There's literally a menu that you pick from, differently priced, different specialities (addiction, trauma, relationship woes, careers guidance, mental health) pictures of the therapist and whether they work in person or online.

Noel seemed good, so I filled in the online enquiry form, and quickly received a text message, lots of fist bump emojis and use of the word 'fella'. Nice, comforting even. We arranged a time to speak on the phone, sure enough, bang on time Noel rang me. We talked briefly about the issues that were concerning me (impending gloom, secondary traumatic stress, never ending internal monologue reminding me of my own mortality), you know the sort of thing. We arranged an appointment for the following week. Noel lived on a sprawling new build estate near a Harvester pub and a Tesco. He'd already told me I could park on his drive. I drove to within a couple of hundred metres of his home and parked up, counting down the few minutes until my earliness could be seen as considerate rather than inconvenient. Noel greeted me with a generous and tight handshake. I was a little uncertain about his wardrobe choice of jogging bottoms and slippers but considered this was probably a projection of my professional standards rather than truly poor conduct. I didn't like it though. It was red flag number one, it would be minimal effort on his part to, to quote Mr Burns from the Simpsons 'throw some jeans on'. I chose to dispense with any awkwardness immediately by handing him the £50 fee before the session started. He showed me into his counselling room; a long room with two wooden framed easy chairs. The laminate floors were standard, there was, and this took me aback a little, a lot of sci fi fan art on the wall and a couple of glass display cabinets with action figures in (mainly Star Wars). You could tell a lot about Noel by his practice room. It was about him, it made me know him and, to be brutally honest, I didn't want to know him or relate to him. I wanted to discuss what was on my mind and never see him again. This immediately drew me out of the zone of therapy and into the zone of consideration of my own practice. I have often given of myself, talked to clients about music, sport, things we've seen on TV, and sometimes even our families. I reflected upon the irony of me objecting to somebody with my own therapeutic style. If that hadn't ruined the 'therapeutic alliance', what happened next blew it clean out of the water and over the hills.

An old friend of mine had recently been diagnosed with a degenerative neurological condition. I'd been to visit him with a friend and to see him unable to walk, feed himself or communicate in more than one or two words had impacted me greatly. I told Noel about this; it wasn't the most significant thing impacting me, but it was the most recent.

"His name's not Jim White, is it?"

Noel asked inquisitively.

"Yeah" I replied, *"Wow, do you know him?"*

I assumed by his response they were friends.

"No, he was a client of mine."

I was dumbstruck. This was a massive breach of confidentiality. Massive. I couldn't believe it. Not only had he totally betrayed my friend's confidence, but he had also acted so unprofessionally that I was taken totally off guard. I challenged Noel on this, he was quick to tell me that my friend was no longer a client and therefore confidentiality no longer applied. I felt physically nauseous. Any professional standards aside, how could I trust a practitioner who had breached confidentiality with such wilful abandonment within minutes of our first meeting? How could I trust him? The answer was obvious, I couldn't.

Noel quickly picked up on my prickly one-word responses to his follow up questions and quickly presented with an anecdote about risk taking, telling me he'd weighed up whether it was appropriate to tell me about my friend to find some common ground or just carry on. It was an interesting attempt at salvaging the relationship, but the damage was done. Noel had, inadvertently, taught me so much about the importance of trust and confidentiality. Brenee Brown talks about earning the right to hear a person's story. Noel had not. He had blown it; he knew he had blown it. The session ended after light conversation interrupted by a barking dog, a window cleaner, an Amazon delivery and the postman. It was a disaster. One that prevented me from accessing therapy again for 18 months.

It also taught me that people are fragile when they access emotional support. I felt uncertain but hopeful of building a safe environment to swim the deepest and most undiscovered waters of my psyche. The confidentiality breach had seen me walk timidly into the daylight, with my hands up protecting my eyes, only to scuttle back into the darkness at speed, whilst my spirit was briefly broken. I indirectly owed Noel a debt of gratitude. I now understood the privilege and enormity of hearing somebody's story. I now understood the importance of my own words, my own expression, and how a fragile therapeutic bond can be shattered with such ease by an ill-thought-out comment or revelation. Noel's lack of consideration reminded me that I could always do better. I left promising to text if I needed

Noel again, but quickly deleted his number. My colleague had told me 75% of therapists shouldn't be in the job. It's not that I didn't believe it, but I had no idea that the truth would come at me with such a prompt and obvious example.

If we're truly on a reflective theme here, there are a few things I regret about my conduct. I didn't walk out of the session there and then as I should have. Neither did I report Noel to the relevant organisation or, and I considered this at length, let Jim's wife know about the breach. I had left others open to access Noel's service, and I left the situation feeling a burden of regret for protecting myself but neglecting my duty of care to others.

Chapter Eight

Ziggy

February 2021

I was lying in bed one sunny Saturday morning when my mobile lit up. It was my friend Jim:

"Hello. Ziggy has asked me for your number, he's getting the band back together from the 90's. It's all good but obviously I didn't want to give your number away without asking you first".

This all dated back about 30 years. I was a 15-year-old kid with a floppy fringe and Doc Marten boots, who loved the local band scene, specifically a local band called The Hillman Avengers. They were all a lot older than me but as a 15-year-old misfit surrounded by rave fans and dance culture, the local band scene provided a place where I belonged and was accepted.

Ziggy was the singer in the Hillman Avengers, I hadn't spoken to him in about 25 years. He was an epic front man, confrontational, a fascinating lyricist and he filled a stage brilliantly. He also had a chronic quarter century addiction to Heroin and a reputation for aggression. He was the loveliest bloke when calm, when not so calm, his reputation for being liberal with his fists travelled far and wide. He was about 5"7 but seemed shorter because a lot of his mates, me included, were above average in height. Whichever period in history you found him in, he would be wearing blue jeans, boots and a biker jacket with his neck length hair slicked back.

I spoke with Ziggy on the phone later that morning. He was funny, charming and complimentary. We talked about the old days, how excited we both were that he was getting the band back together for one night only, how Jim was making an excellent replacement bass player for the lineup, and generally how thrilled we both were at the prospect of getting the old gang back together. I pinged him twenty pounds for tickets and looked forward to our big night out in a few months' time. The occasional text message floated back and forth for a day or two. It was a pleasant reunion. The months rolled by with Jim sending me occasional band rehearsal updates and even a photo of me and Ziggy at a Hillman Avengers gig about 30 years previously. Then the enthusiasm seemed to die down a bit, the updates dried up and life went on as normal.

Three months later I attended my normal community multi-disciplinary meeting. This is basically a get together of community doctors, nurses, physios and occupational therapists to discuss community patients and consider anyone in need of admission to the inpatient unit. Before I went to the meeting, I checked the list of names to be discussed. One name leapt out at me, Mark Green. I checked the address. The address listed was somewhere near where he lived. The familiar feeling of stomach churning, rush of blood to the head. It couldn't be. It just couldn't be. It was Ziggy. I needed to find out without breaching any confidentiality, so I sent a text to Jim:

"Alright Jim, bit of a random one, are you still rehearsing with The Hillman Avengers?" I asked just before getting in the car for the drive to the meeting at the hospice.

"Hello mate. No, not since second lockdown, I don't think that's going to happen now, Ziggy is seriously ill" he replied.

So, there it was. All the confirmation I needed.

I told Jim I was sorry to hear the news but was careful not to disclose that I knew anything about it. I wanted to be a good friend, but that was trumped by being a good social worker. It's never easy, and sometimes you can feel like a right smug know-it-all when you have information but you're unwilling to disclose it.

I walked the short distance through the hospice from the car park largely unaware of the ambience. I sat in the meeting, numbly autopiloting the small talk with the community team and waited impatiently and fidgeting to hear about what was happening. I listened as they described him; decades of class A drug abuse, musician, married with three grown up kids, all the stuff that I knew but I was still hoping I had made a mistake. It was him, and they were bringing him in for symptom control.

Seeing somebody you know for the first time in hospice care is an emotionally wrenching thing for those who have a comfort zone. You have no idea if the person you are about to see is as you remember them, or physically changed. Diseases that bring a person into end-of-life care can have a shocking impact on the look of a person. The disease and accompanying treatments can lead to weight loss, weight gain, swelling, hair loss and changes in physical colour just to name a few. There could also be physical symptoms of tumours or growths. Factoring in that I hadn't seen Ziggy in about 25 years I had no idea what to expect. I put on my gloves, apron and mask and made my way to the Inpatient Unit.

I knocked on the door and went in. Ziggy's daughter and wife were visibly distressed, busily folding clothes and arranging bedding. Ziggy's daughter was a lady of early twenties, long dark hair, leggings and a long-hooded sweatshirt. She was occupying herself and visibly trying not to cry. Ziggy's wife stood looking dumbstruck in the corner in a flowing tartan dress and big black boots. She had long grey hair with streaks of colour. Ziggy was as I remembered him, but much thinner. His disease had deprived him of his ability to digest food and drink so now all nutrition was going straight into his stomach via a peg. He lay in bed in a hospital gown fidgeting with his phone and trying to get comfortable. The collection of tubes attached to his nose, stomach and wrist were clearly causing agitation.

I introduced myself firstly to the family:

"Hi, my name is Andy, I'm the social worker on duty today, but Ziggy knows me better as Rooky". Rooky was my nickname as a child.

"ROOOOKKKKKYYYYYY, hello mate! Fucking hell, I owe you £20!"

"Hiya mate, no worries lad, you don't owe me anything."

We talked a while, and Ziggy talked to his wife and daughter about the times we had shared some 30 years previous. I showed Ziggy's wife and daughter the photo of me in a mosh pit at Ziggy's gig, they had a sense of relief and elation that within an hour of hospice admission, there was an old friend showing his face. It made things known, ok, safe.

I excused myself as the family were busy, but promised to visit again the next day when everything had settled down a bit and Ziggy had found his bearings.

"Is there anything I can do for you? Anything you need?" I asked.

"Oh yes please mate, can you just ring Ian, Del, Jonesy and Jim, let them know I'm here and what's going on".

"Sure, mate no worries at all. Anything you need me tell them specifically?".

"Tell them they're my brothers and I love them" replied Ziggy, he looked at me and smiled.

I was so glad he asked me to do this. It meant I could call and update them, without any need for secrecy. I left the ward and checked my watch, my afternoon shift had long since finished and the sun was taking it's leave into the early springtime dusk.

Ian was Ziggy's oldest and closest friend, and guitarist in the Hillman Avengers:

"Hello?"

"Alright mate, it's Rooky, how you're doing?"

"Bloody hell mate, long time no see, how you doing?"

"I'm good thanks mate. Listen, I'm not sure if you knew but I'm a social worker at the hospice. Ziggy is here as a patient; I've just been to visit him and asking me to let you know that you're his brother and he loves you".

Silence.

"Oh, mate thank you" said Ian with genuine relief "I had no idea where he was. I've been trying to ring all of them for days. I'm just glad he's safe".

We talked a short while, I hadn't spoken to Ian for a couple of years so tinged as it was by sorrow, the conversation was filled with nostalgia and laughter. I called the others as requested, the responses were as I expected: emotional, sad, grateful and reflective.

The following day I went to see Ziggy again. I saw a meme on social media that said: "There is no part of the nursing degree that prepares you for the amount of deathbed murder confessions you will hear". It was funny, but also carried a truth for which I was ill-prepared. It was Ziggy's second day in the Hospice, so I went to check in and see how he was doing.

Ziggy had, like many other people, seen hospice admission as a finale to his life and having discovered God in recent months, had found cause to seek mercy for his sins. He'd been a Heroin addict for almost his entire adult life. His home was almost completely empty of comfort or luxury items. His family had become accustomed to him selling whatever family possessions carried any value to buy drugs throughout his life. They had long since learned to keep any valuable possessions or keepsakes in secret, under lock and key, as they would soon be taken and cashed in for narcotics before their absence had even been noted.

Ziggy was open, realistic and hopeful about his situation. He was unapologetic and saw the aggressive and burrowing cancer that was ravaging him as penance for a life spent on the cycle of using, craving, buying, foraging and excusing that so many addicts do, or as he once told Jim:

"I've burned a hole in my soul with the junk".

I have long chosen to view addiction as a disease. Mainly because the only other real alternative to this is choice. As a recovering alcoholic myself, I refuse to believe that somebody would choose addiction. It dominates your thoughts, motivates your actions, enslaves you and constantly batters at your morality until the abnormal becomes normal, the despicable becomes the acceptable, and the rancid becomes the chosen. As Brandon Novak so succinctly puts it: "it's nothing personal, just business". Addicts don't choose to hurt their families and loved ones, it's just any obstacles to that addiction must go. If you stand in the way of the addict and their fix, you'll get hurt, no matter how much you love the addict, or the addict loves you. Addicts don't think with clarity, expanse or logic. If we reflect on it, any smoker who bought a packet of cigarettes would look at the images of brown teeth, black lungs, warnings about impotence, early death, potential amputations and decide, with no great prompting to never smoke again. I like Subway sandwiches, but if I thought for a New York second that eating Subway sandwiches would give me erectile disfunction, rancid teeth, breath that smelt like a dead rat in a drainpipe and an early death, I'd be abandoning the local Subway franchise and off to the local supermarket chain for a meal deal before you could say 'loyalty card'. That's the addicted mind, it constantly adjusts and depletes to incorporate acquisition and ingestion of whatever it is addicted to.

I walked into Ziggy's room, and he bid me good morning. He was sat up in bed, visibly thin and without much colour. We talked a while, about mutual friends, music, politics, but it was clear that this was just a warmup to the main event. Ziggy talked about being hungry. He had long since received all his meals through a tube as he was no longer able to chew, swallow or digest his food.

"Mate if I could do anything in the world right now, I'd go to Burger King. I haven't eaten in six weeks I'm starving".

Ziggy suddenly understood the joys of little things. A walk in the park, a meal out, time with his kids, a new album by a favourite band. Then he handed me a book.

"Would you mind reading something to me mate?" he asked handing me a book.

"Psalm 23:1–64 Yea, though I walk through the valley of the shadow of death, I will fear no evil: for thou art with me; thy rod and thy staff they comfort me."

For that moment he was not Ziggy, and I was not me. He was not a patient, and I was not a social worker. We were just two people connected by words and reflection. I read and talked slowly. I could see that in this moment, there was no more important thing in the world than the words we were sharing. And there it was again, the sense of privilege. A man who had lived 53 years was coming to the end of his life. Not a beat had been missed in 53 years and now that heart was due to stop forever.

Alcoholics Anonymous and Narcotics Anonymous normally work with God. Ziggy crossed the finish line flanked by God on one side and addiction on the other. He had taken solace and comfort from both at different times of his life, and he had never found the clarity or penance that sobriety brings to the few addicts who seek it out.

"Thou preparest a table before me in the presence of mine enemies: thou anointest my head with oil; my cup runneth over."

I finished the passage and sat on the chair next to Ziggy's bed. We had a moment of silence.

"Brilliant, cheers mate, appreciate that" he said smiling with utmost sincerity.

"Anything else I can do for you?"

"Have you got ten minutes? I need to tell somebody something".

Ziggy had a past. There was no doubting that, but even this caught me off guard.

"It was about 1984. I was working at the old printshop on Grahamsley Street. I'd just finished the late shift, so it would've been about 2am. In the shadows I saw some lads, could've been 3, maybe 5, just between the Fleece pub and the park. That was my way home and I really didn't fancy it, so I decided to walk up the High Street and take another route. Anyway, as soon as they saw me, they started to follow me, you know how it is. I sped up, I could hear them behind me, I started to run then they started chasing me. So, by this stage I'm running for my life. I peg it up Jackson Street and I'm done. I couldn't run any more. I checked my pockets for something, anything. I'd got a Stanley I used for opening boxes and whatever. I figured I can just wave it about and they'll back off, but by the time I've bent over and tried to get my breath. The first one of them was a few feet away. He wasn't big, but he was fit, and the others had been left behind. He saw that it was just him and me and he panicked and before you know it, we were face to face, both out of breath and staring eye to eye. He was a local bloke, smart trousers, black shoes, suit jacket, Flock of Seagulls haircut and all that nonsense. I could see his mates were gaining on me, so I pulled the knife and just swung it. It sliced him right across the face and he immediately doubled over. I should've run. Call it adrenalin, call it red mist I don't know, but I take advantage of him being bent over and just stuck it as hard as I could into his side. I could see his hands were covered in blood, his mates were gaining on me, and he immediately hit the floor."

"I ran. I wasn't out of breath anymore. I ran and ran for about 20 minutes through parks and backstreets. After about half an hour I could hear sirens in the distance; Ambulance, Police you name it. Eventually I got back to my bedsit, having gone about 3 or 4 miles out of the way. I locked the door and slumped down by it to block it, but I was exhausted, I couldn't move. I stayed there for hours".

Ziggy went on to tell me about how he sat and waited, then how he continued to live and work with a semblance of routine whilst permanently listening out for sirens, knocks at the door and revenge attacks. Ziggy didn't know if the man he stabbed died, and he wouldn't have been able to pick any of them out of a line-up. But this made him fear everyone and everything. One day, at some point, the Police would come or some family member with a grudge, probably in the dead of night. Like treacle in an hourglass, the thoughts, the guilt and the fear gradually dripped away. But Ziggy had already established by this point that use of substances was a way to sleep and forget and, to use his words; 'shut the voices up'.

As he told me the story, my perception of Ziggy changed. He was unapologetic but he wanted to be heard. He wanted to share his stories and his life. And despite my belief that I was a practitioner that used unconditional positive regard and non-judgment as I had been taught, for the first time I saw the man, not just the addict. Ziggy was sleepy by this point, so I left him to rest. I was on leave the following day, Friday, so promised I would drop by on Monday morning.

I always carry guilt for taking annual leave at times like this, but burnout will hit you fast if you don't take it. I knew there was more Ziggy wanted to tell me but now wasn't the time. Through medication, progressive disease and the excess of his revelation, he had exhausted himself. I had a restful couple of days off. On Sunday morning I went downstairs to put the kettle on and saw my laptop on the table. I flicked it on just to check.

Ziggy had died. I couldn't check his record, that wouldn't be an appropriate thing to do on a day off for nothing more than personal enquiry, but the gravestone icon next to his name on the patient list told me all I needed to know. He had died in the early hours of that morning. I gazed at the screen for a while, lost in the moment, then lost in professional conflict. I couldn't let anybody know; nobody had consented to me letting Ziggy's friends know he had died. As much as I fancied myself as going a bit rogue every now and again, the family may have decided not to break the news yet. Maybe one of his kids didn't have mobile signal and didn't want to read about his dad's death on Facebook. There were lots of maybes floating about in my head, but they all led me to the conclusion that I needed to keep this to myself until I knew it was common knowledge and the family had made the decision to put the news into the public domain.

I went for a walk to think and process the news. It was a fresh, cold morning with a clear blue sky. The nighttime frost made the grass crunch as I walked leaving a line of footprints. I found a bench and sat. I was sorry that Ziggy had maybe taken something to death that he might have wanted to share. Maybe I could've gone in on my day off for an hour. It would have set a pretty dangerous precedent from a wellbeing perspective, but maybe we could've got more time to talk. Maybe his family would've been there, and he wouldn't have wanted to see me. Maybe he'd have been asleep. That whole experience taught me something, ifs, buts, shoulds and maybes aren't helpful. Expectations are, to quote Anne Lamott, 'resentments under construction'.

And so, I forgave myself, not for the first time, not for the last time. I could've done more, but then I suppose I could've done less too. I couldn't have changed anything, and I was going by the assumption that Ziggy did have something else to tell me. I didn't know this to be the case. There were plenty of other people who could've given emotional support and spoken to him, although I didn't shoulder this burden alone, I assumed responsibility for loyalty to my friends.

As I managed to reason myself into submission and conclude that my conscience was clear, I had a moment of calm. I sat in the park, crunchy frozen grass beneath my feet, reflecting that I was so glad that I'd had the interactions that I'd had, that Ziggy had planned the gig, got in touch, that I'd managed to see him in the hospice and share those conversations with him. I decided the best course of action now would be silence. In a day or two the news would be out that Ziggy had died. I decided this would be a straightforward course of action - do nothing and wait. Just as I drew my conclusions, a voiced called my name. A silhouette walked toward me eclipsed by the morning sun.

Del was a nice guy but the person I wanted to see least in the world in this light and on this morning, he was an old friend of Ziggy's. They had played in bands together for years and I knew them both well after many years of just being around. I was hoping for small talk. I'm not a big fan of small talk but it wouldn't take Del long to put two and two together and realise that I probably knew what was going on. He didn't beat about the bush.

Del had been a phenomenal drummer in his youth. He'd gone bald in the later stages of high school and had always kept a freshly shaved head since. He was short but in all the time I'd known him he'd always dressed immaculately, usually in a suit and tie. He'd been a popular figure around the pubs and bars in town, but the years hadn't been kind to him. Years of smoking forty cigarettes a day had left him wheezy. He had several teeth missing giving him a light but notable lisp. The teeth he did have were yellowed by years of abuse, but his smile was still glorious.

"Have you heard about Ziggy?" he began.

A simple question, but one that presented me with a dilemma. I didn't want to be a smug, secretive, I-know-and-you-don't arsehole, but neither did I want to go spouting personal news when the family hadn't had the chance to announce it in their own way.

"Jim told me he wasn't well."

"Yeah, Cancer"

"I'm sorry to hear that man" I said, in the vague hope we might be able to totally forget about it and change the subject.

"He's in hospital, I'll probably get up there and see him in the week."

The internal conflict was gnarly, but the consequence inevitable. For reasons of confidentiality and respect for the family, I had to have a conversation with Del based on a significant and brutal mistruth. Ziggy wasn't in the hospital; he was at the hospice. He had died and his body was now in the mortuary there. We talked a little longer.

He talked about hoping Ziggy would be well again soon, how he hoped the reunion gig would still happen and of other things that might happen that I knew never would. This was professional conflict at its most absolute. I was desperate to tell Del but knew I couldn't. I knew I was doing the right thing not telling him but allowing him to talk about plans with a mate I knew had died felt so wrong. We went our separate ways shortly after.

Two days later a mutual friend called me. He said how grateful everybody had been for the care and support Ziggy and his family had received. Evidently my conscience was not as clear as I thought as I explained to him how sorry I was that I couldn't let him know he'd died as soon as I knew. They all knew it was the right thing to do, as did I. I settled after this conversation, making peace with the fact that there would always be times where doing the right thing wouldn't feel comfortable, where I would have to say 'sorry, I'm not allowed to tell you' like some sort of jobsworth school prefect with a finger to his lips.

Sometimes doing the right thing just doesn't sit well and we must make decisions that take us firmly away from our comfort zone. On this occasion it was in one of those awful moments where personal life and hospice life collide. Your present is suddenly in the company of your past, and people, issues and stories that you'd hitherto compartmentalised mix together. Then you remember that, in fact, there is death involved, and nobody is giving you a second thought. When Del found out later that day that Ziggy had died, there is no chance he would've even considered that I'd known and chose not to tell him, nobody would be sitting at home saying awful things about me because they didn't find out about Ziggy's death until the family were ready to tell them. The reality is that this was the job, the parameters of confidentiality are clearly set. Only a sociopath or a narcissist would think announcing a death before a family had time to do it would be acceptable behaviour. So, there we are, nagging doubts aside, unnecessary forgiveness obtained, a social work intervention done by the book. The nagging doubt that I could've done more faded with time. I guess that's what makes a good professional regardless of your job or discipline. If you genuinely care about what you're doing and who you're doing it with, you'll always wish you could've done more.

Mercifully, Ziggy's funeral, to which I was invited during the Covid lockdown, didn't reflect any of the chaos of his life. Those who weren't invited attended to stand outside, and any gripes or grievances between the attendees (and there were many) were left in the amnesty box of decency for the duration of the ceremony.

I was grateful and humbled to be invited to the funeral when other friends had not been, not for any reason of selfishness or one upmanship you understand. I saw it as a personal validation of my interventions when I was working. The family took the time out to tell me how much they had appreciated Ziggy's time in the hospice. From a life of addiction, of empty rooms, sold possessions and phone calls from debt chasing dealers, he had found peace, or maybe in the manner of how he was referred in for hospice care, peace had found him. The hospice was a haven, not just for Ziggy, but for those who cared about him and wished that his crippling addiction could've been overcome yet bore him no blame. After 30 years of the trauma of seeing someone they loved unconditionally making decision after decision that hurt them psychologically, and him absolutely, he was safe. He was serene, elevated by his love for God, calm in the belief that his disease and forthcoming premature death were fair cost for not making the most of God's gifts. For the first time, sanctuary had found him and carried him restfully away from the enemy he had made in himself.

When I think back to how this affected me and those around me, I am overwhelmed by my good fortune that meant I could make a difference. Ziggy's family told me how relieved they felt that a friendly face had made them feel so at ease within moments of their arrival at the hospice. This was not by design, it was my luck and theirs that I was in that meeting, on that day, seeing that list of names. I felt blessed to have seen Ziggy in those final days, heard his stories and shared in his unique view of the world. He was a fascinating and insightful man. He was testament to the fact that addiction doesn't see social class, income, religion, creativity or responsibility. It just sees the one mistake of the person who in a dark or naïve moment uses for the first time and becomes afflicted with addiction for the rest of their days. Behind the addiction was an intelligent, loving, caring man. His adult children took turns at his funeral sharing how creative and committed he was as a father. This was the man I saw in the hospice. It was a gift to hear those stories, but an infinitely greater gift to know that he was now at peace.

Chapter Nine

Intermission- Making Death Amazing

The longer I have worked in palliative care, the more I have had to accept the realities of death and dying. The more you reflect and consider things, the more your thinking on the matter evolves and grows. It's ok for me, I have had far more time to think about it than most. I've seen good deaths, bad deaths, surprise deaths, expected deaths, well planned deaths and deaths cloaked in denial.

I often experience the families of patients who, although they are in possession of all the facts, refuse to believe that a family member is dying. This sets back the emotional support process by some way. The reality is, we cannot support somebody if they don't know the facts or are simply refusing to believe them. And why don't they believe them? For the most part the answer is simple. Fear. When we really dig deep and unpack the emotional journey of either a person coming to the end of the life, or one of their loved ones, there is often so much fear. The fears can be legion, fear of being forgotten, of partners moving on a little too quickly and meeting somebody new, of missing out on a significant life event or, of actual death itself. This is notwithstanding the fire and brimstone folk who believe that their very existence is something that should be forgiven, either by way of indoctrination in a faith or some rather irksome family dynamics. It struck me after long hours processing and trying to come up with a solution that our very perception of death might need to change in order to help us process what is inevitable. Funerals could be a day of congratulation, of celebration, of saying thank you to a person for the immense contribution they have made with their lives. If we could remove that element of fear and change our perception, and perhaps see it as us crossing the finish line rather than being 'lost', perhaps our entire outlook might change. We are still bogged down in historic dogma when it comes to death. If it is as inevitable as birth, we should consider altering our perception and approach to lose the fear.

The one question that gets asked of palliative care professionals more than any other is the 'what to say?' question. Some people are fixers, they want to find a solution, but there are no solutions here. Some people want to offer consolation. Again, there is no consolation here. This is a major problem for people who are uncomfortable with silence. Our unilateral British fear of silence can lead us down rabbit holes it is difficult to U-turn out of. I supported a young lady who, at her husband's funeral, was told by an older lady:

"Don't worry, you're young and pretty enough to meet somebody new".

This was tactless, insensitive, you name it. But the reality was that it probably came from a misguided attempt at compassion or comfort. Many people fear silence, much like they fear being unseen. For many a bad connection or interaction is better than no connection at all. I remember being with one client who had massively insulted her carer who had a large red birthmark on her face. Something of the "you'd be so pretty if you didn't have that on your face" nature of comment. I remember asking him what he was thinking. He was a northerner rattling off the old 'say as I find it, speak my mind' clichés. Then he turned the conversation over to me:

"What am I supposed to say, that it wouldn't bother me, that I think she's attractive with it?".

"Well...", I replied with caution, *"You could just say nothing"*.

We sat for a moment of silence. It genuinely seemed as though he had never considered that option before. The world is full of social media, pictures, blogging, online newspapers with comment sections, many of which have turned into poisonous and venous cesspits of ill-thought out, bigoted tripe that serves no purpose other than to show the author as a coward and an ignoramus. So, here's the big revelation: when we're supporting people pre or post bereavement, a family member, somebody with a diagnosis, anyone, we need to listen. Most people who have a disease or a recently deceased relative don't need pearls of wisdom. If I'm supporting a person who hasn't slept in weeks due to grief, fear or anxiety, the chances of me saying the first thing that comes into my head, and that thing being such a zinger that it immediately solves the problem, is highly remote.

We need to overcome our fear of social discomfort and just sit in silence when it is required. If there is no consolation, no cure, no solution, nothing we can say that will help, then silence is undeniably better than saying something counter-productive. I have said on so many occasions that 90% of my job is just showing up for people and listening to them. It sounds like I'm being self-depreciating. Granted, the other 10% is courage, vulnerability, experience, knowledge and qualification. But what works, and what really matters, is the power to listen without judgment, without interruption and without waiting to speak. I'm not going to play down how incredibly difficult this is to attain, especially for somebody like me, who can talk incessantly on any number of topics. But so often, the people we support don't want a solution; they want to be heard and validated. Sometimes, as with our men's group, just knowing you're not alone is enough to keep the world just manageable enough to fight on for one more day. Teachers often talk to me about the challenges of supporting a bereaved child and how helpless they feel. I always offer the same response. You are offering a consistent, safe, structured environment to a young person in a time of uncertainty and chaos. Turning up and doing what you always do is the best gift you can give to a huge number of bereaved children; children who just need to know the world is still turning and the sun will come up in the morning.

The challenge with supporting people in such heightened emotional states is that the fears and distress are all rational. As emotional supporters, we can't find solutions, we can't find cures. But what we can do, with careful and structured support is restore hope to people who feel like they have lost all of theirs.

Chapter Ten

Geoff

August 2020

"I think the best thing for me would be to kill myself".

That was the line. A line that ordinarily would leave me in a flurry of panic and paperwork, but not today.

Geoff was somebody I'd known through the hospice for about 18 months. His wife had died there the previous year, and now his own diagnosis of head and neck cancer was fast progressing. Geoff was a pragmatic, surly but incredibly likeable man. His wife Nancy was in a similar mould. We had some wonderful and enlightening conversations when she was receiving end of life care at the hospice. Likewise, she wasn't backwards at coming forwards when it came to kicking me out her room because she wanted to watch Cash in The Attic. I met Geoff when Nancy was in the hospice.

"I'll have to warn you", said the ward sister, "He's a grumpy sod and he's upset a lot of the staff".

His apparent surliness was perceived to be a coping strategy to enable him to manage the imminent death of his wife. I found him to be otherwise. He was a realistic, highly intelligent senior manager who had made a great deal of waves in the construction industry. He had fascinating insights into politics, current affairs and the problem with the health service. Any suggestion that Geoff had been a little too direct, or a little too assertive was met with the same response:

"It's nothing personal, just business".

When Nancy died Geoff was expectedly practical. The funeral was short, and at its conclusion Geoff disappeared out of the front door of the crematorium, turned his phone off, and went home asking not to be disturbed for a few days.

Just over a year later I took a call from our contact centre.

"A patient has just called in asking to speak to you".

"Can I take their name?"

The call taker told me his name, how unwell he was becoming, and how isolated he had become because he had "literally upset everyone he has come into contact with".

I called Geoff immediately:

"Andy" Geoff barked enthusiastically, "How are you doing Buddy?"

I was genuinely taken aback by his enthusiasm and warmth. Geoff's voice was husky due a lack of saliva, he was uncertain as to whether this was due to his disease or his intensive radiotherapy. However, Geoff was able to paint a vivid picture of craving fish and chips but finding that all food just blended into a dry and tasteless ball in his mouth. As a result, Geoff lived off nutrition shakes that had led to him losing significant amounts of weight. I'd never known 19 stone Geoff, I'd only known 12 stone Geoff, so seeing him didn't have that shocking impact of seeing him looking thin.

Geoff still stood at 6"1 and cut a dominating figure. His tall gait and short neatly trimmed hair depicted a man of discipline in the face of trauma. His dry throat barked his words, and he constantly sipped a plastic bottle of water to keep his mouth lubricated.

Geoff lived, now alone, in a new build bungalow on a neat but well to do housing estate on the nicer side of town. He gave me the tour, he'd reworked his entire garden with a water feature, rockery and blooming roses. In the corner of the garden was a brand-new park bench with a small brass plaque:

"In memory of Nancy. My soul mate and my everything."

This was a romantic and disarming gesture from a man who never removed his emotional armour. My perceptions changed in that moment. It occurred to me that his reworking of his home was preparing it for sale by his family after his death. The bench with the plaque was a memorial that said more to me about his love for Nancy than any words he had ever spoken in my presence. He loved and missed her unconditionally, and that love continued after her death.

Whilst Geoff was a brilliant and articulate man, able to talk about a plethora of fascinating subjects, any such emotional discussion led Geoff to the same conclusion every time:

"Ah well, that's how it is."

As we went back into the house, Geoff asked me to sit down and plumped down on the sofa adjacent to me.

"I think the best thing for me would be to kill myself".

I've attended many education sessions on suicide ideation and suicide prevention. The vast majority of these courses approach the subject from the angle of mental health. That is, anyone who is suicidal has poor mental health, therefore, if we support this person to have improved mental health then they will no longer be suicidal and that would be a positive outcome.

Geoff knew this. He knew my initial response would be the suicide prevention angle, and he was quick to head me off at the pass.

"I know you're going to try and talk me out of it. But look at it like this, my wife was my soul mate, we had 55 wonderful, glorious years together. And now she's gone. My kids have grown up and left home, they live miles away, I rarely see them". I tried to interject.

"There's no misery here Buddy. Don't worry. I've had a long life, I've seen the world, I've raised children, I've earned well, I've achieved a lot."

We sat in silence. I was ever so slightly stunned. Even by Geoff's standards this was frank.

"…and now it's over" he continued.

Every core of my being wanted to explain to Geoff that there was still something for him to live for, but I understood. He was a proud man, he had harnessed control, management and assertiveness over every aspect of his life since adulthood started some 57 years ago. Now he was losing control of his body, his balance, his organs, and he wanted to take control back.

"I'm thinking pills" he croaked firmly.

I was stunned into a conversational submission. Lost. The silence was uncharacteristically panic inducing, and I asked the only question I could think of.

"What do you have?"

"Well," Geoff replied assertively, like he was delivering a change management seminar, which he kind of was, "I'm nearly out of cancer drugs but I'm stocked up on Nancy's old anti-depressants". He was clearly unflapped by my question. I surmised this was probably a reflection of how well he knew and trusted me. We quickly concluded that anti-depressants wouldn't kill him. They'd make him feel groggy for a few days, but it wouldn't be fatal.

"Ah, Fuck" sighed Geoff slumping back into his easy chair, "Can't get a break at the moment".

We both laughed, Geoff raucously, me nervously, at the sheer absurdity of how quickly our conversation had escalated. I sat forward and aimed my gaze towards Geoff.

"Geoff". I whispered, catching his eye, *"Not tonight, eh? See how you feel tomorrow"*.

Geoff smiled and sighed.

I wanted to be there for him. I understood how he felt, or more accurately, I think I would feel the same in his position. There was nothing morose about Geoff, he just knew that the wonderful life as he knew it was over, he'd reflected on what his life had become since his wife had died and wasn't accepting of it. I had no reason to doubt Geoff's mental capacity to make a decision. Although preservation of life is deep rooted in the principles of what we do, so is offering choice, as is promotion of dignity. Geoff didn't feel dignified any more. Had he have been able to live healthily maybe he would have found greater purpose, found joy in food, drink or a new hobby. Had Nancy still have been alive he would've had the consistent and loving partnership he had become accustomed to without ever taking it for granted.

Geoff had weighed up the pros and cons with great logic and consideration. He knew what his options were and understood his preferences. I was doubtless that he didn't lack the courage to kill himself. I left Geoff alone at home. He seemed relieved to have shared the goings on in his psyche and promised me he wouldn't kill himself that night.

"Don't worry", he said as I left his house and he walked me to the door, "I won't give you any more unnecessary paperwork to do" he said, presumably referring to the hospice's rigid incident reporting policy.

Geoff's was my last visit of the day, and I felt like there was something very unresolved about our conversation. Perhaps it was that Geoff joked about staying alive to prevent giving me extra work, not because he wanted to stay alive. I vowed to call him the following day to check in and maybe talk more about how he was feeling. I knew this was a tall order. Geoff was a closed book most of the time emotionally speaking.

The following day, my phone was ringing as soon as I turned it on. Geoff had had a bad night. He had called our contact centre distressed with chest pains. I had other appointments to do that morning but scheduled to call Geoff in the afternoon. The call centre manager asked me if I could possibly check in with him. When the time came, I checked our system and saw that three different health professionals had called Geoff for various reasons that day, he'd been unwell and agitated. One call was the check in, but the other two calls were scheduled from departments who didn't know the other was calling. My major uncertainty was that if Geoff was annoyed by the amount of contact today, would he perceive my call as a helpful opportunity to summarise the events of the day? Or would he perceive me as just another meddler? Geoff's direct and pragmatic nature was, as always, a reliable spirit level to judge my uncertainty.

"Oh Andy, not now, Fuck off alright?".

I was in little doubt after that. I wasn't surprised. Geoff had made clear his intentions and I'm sure viewed the various health interventions of the day as merely prolonging the life he no longer wanted. I knew Geoff. I knew how he was and how he was feeling, so I didn't take his response too personally, as he knew I wouldn't. I put a note in my diary to call him in a few days when he would hopefully have calmed down a little.

The following afternoon I took a call from Geoff's son. He had gone to bed the previous night and died peacefully and naturally in his sleep. My initial response was conflicted. I offered my condolences which were warmly received with a thank you for keeping an eye on Geoff. I knew he'd simply got to the end of being alive and had had enough.

The time was right for him. I was partly troubled by a positive therapeutic relationship reaching its conclusion with me being told to fuck off, but that was Geoff. He was uncompromising, strong of character and direct. His son was kind enough to tell me how helpful his dad had found our conversations. He concluded by politely telling me that there was no need for me to attend Geoff's funeral. Geoff had made quite clear, family only, no hymns, no readings, just get the job done and everyone can go. I smiled when I heard this. It is rare that my line of work brings absolute closure or certainty, but this did. I knew these were Geoff's final wishes and I could almost hear him saying it. Geoff died peacefully, with dignity, and when he wanted, and leaving wishes for a funeral that was understated and modest. Nothing personal, just business.

Chapter Eleven

An apology to Brianna

August 2018

Through this book I hope I have constructed a narrative of humility and vulnerability. Partially, it is a fact that we get things wrong. In palliative care, whether we are supporting a patient, a family member or a client, the stakes are high. Nobody wants to be the anecdotal example of poor or careless practice, or much worse the subject of a Daily Mail article. And yet here we are, vulnerable every day, in every call, visit or appointment. There is always the possibility of putting one's foot in it. So much in social work education is about the 'use of self'. If, like me, you're somebody who attempts humour or light heartedness to defuse difficult situations, then palliative care social work is at best a bit of a cauldron.

The occasion that leaps to mind when I think of this (and when I say 'leap to mind' I mean 'still keeps me awake to this day'), is Brianna.

Brianna was allocated to me for bereavement support. Her husband had died in hospice care after several years of progressive illness. I called and arranged a visit agreeing to see her at work where she was the CEO. Upon arriving at her office building, I could tell Brianna held some significant authority in the company she managed. The office was a bleak 1970's greying building in a bleak greying corner of a bleak greying East Midlands industrial estate. I had to loop around the blocks of anonymous, symmetrical industrial units interspersed with the odd sandwich bar for about three laps. Eventually I found a map that showed me that Brianna's company was ensconced around the back of another pretty much identical unit.

I parked up and walked towards the building. In social work you see much that is bleak and dystopian. Nothing paints a picture more greying and grimmer, more 'Lowry' than a 1970's industrial estate. As a good social worker, I needed to keep my judgements to myself, but this place had the musty funk of the timesheets, name tags and data entry of the temp jobs I undertook in my directionless twenties. I was already on the back foot. Unfortunately, it was a recall to a period of my life where I was relieved of several opportunities when I 'lacked direction' and routinely told line managers of similar age to myself to go fuck themselves if they thought they could find somebody better than me. So, there I was, reminiscent of so many professional failures, unbeknown to me that I was about to commit the latest.

I spoke to the receptionist and was soon ushered forth into Brianna's office where she offered me a firm handshake and thanked me for coming. We sat opposite each other in the breakout area of her office. Brianna was an elegant lady in her late 50's. She dressed in a fitted burgundy trouser suit, with dark hair in a practical bob and the tanned complexion of a person who was as well travelled as she was influential. I introduced myself to Brianna and asked her an easy opening question about how work was, which she totally ignored. There was something Brianna wanted to talk about, my questions wouldn't be needed any time soon. Brianna pulled out a very robust ring binder. It was indexed with dividers and Polly Pockets, the full nine yards. She dropped the ring binder on the table, creating a sort of loud 'doosh' noise.

"He was a common-sense man my husband" Brianna began sullenly with a Celtic brogue. I could tell by some of paraphernalia around her office she was an Ulsterwoman (one plaque, one postcard on the wall, one Ireland rugby scarf draped over a bookshelf). I could also tell that Brianna was not in the mood for small talk.

"Look at this" she said pushing the folder towards me. I opened it up and inside was possibly the most well organised and complete ring binder I'd ever seen. Everything Brianna would possibly need was in it.

"It's all here" Brianna said knowingly soliciting an awkward silence from me, "life insurance, house insurance, bank accounts, pin numbers, passwords, funeral planning, even the code for the burglar alarm at home. Everything, he's thought of everything". I was sensing a 'but' as we sat in silence. On this day, for whatever reason, I wasn't comfortable so took the plunge:

"I'm sensing a 'but' here Brianna".

"Would it have fucking hurt him to say, 'I love you'?" She snapped.

"Everything. He thought of everything. He even wrote down when the fucking bins go out. He wrote down the pin number to the Sky box, the wireless code, the Tesco Clubcard is in there. Three words. Three fucking words. I. Love. You."

Brianna's momentum didn't stumble as tears streamed down her face smudging her eye makeup.

"Yes brilliant. He was practical, he took care of things I don't have to worry about money or the house or when to use my Clubcard points. But why couldn't he fucking write 'I love you' on one of those millions of pieces of fucking A4 that he spent so long curating".

My heart broke for her. This was a strong woman, an assertive and dominant business career, and a husband who lived with a terminal prognosis for four long years, a man who, remembering the smaller details, had managed to neglect the three words which mattered most to his wife of 30 years. I reflected on the early judgments I had made about Brianna, assuming that this closed off, almost military of people would appreciate the practical approach. I dug deep, making the same mistake I'd made several times before. I tried to find consolation or a solution.

"Maybe this was his way of saying that" I offered. *"Maybe he thought doing all this was his way of showing that he loved you and he'd thought about your welfare".*

This was a rooky error. Brianna's husband had died three weeks ago, she was given the folder by the care staff at the hospice and had three weeks to read, peruse, reflect and consider her reaction. She'd had three weeks to think about it and little else, and I, rather obnoxiously thought that the first thought that popped into my head might be the thought that changed the game. I was wrong, and Brianna was agitated by my response. Brianna had her head in her hands with tears and sniffles audible through her fingers.

"So" she replied raising her head, showing red eyes, blurred make up and ruffled hair "he was so busy putting together his fucking binder that he couldn't find the time to write three words" she said, clearly rattled, "that's just fucking great, thanks for clearing that up".

I whispered an apology while Brianna composed herself and vowed that this time, I would keep my stupid mouth firmly shut until I could say something relatively well thought out or helpful. Brianna was aware I was on the back foot and immediately responded.

"I'm sorry", she whispered. "I'm just angry. I'm angry at the situation, I'm angry at my friend's whose husbands haven't died, I'm angry at elderly couples on the street who have had the chance to grow old together, I'm angry at myself for feeling such shitty things about people who have done nothing wrong, I'm angry at my kids for getting on with their lives and going back to work. But", Brianna stopped, gazed out of the office window into the carpark, "I'm just so fucking angry at Andrew for dying. How crazy is that? He had fucking Cancer; he didn't want to die. He didn't smoke, he drank with infuriating restraint. He did everything with infuriating restraint." The angrier Brianna got, the thicker and broader her Ulster accent became.

"Why me?" Brianna was starting to raise her voice now. A couple of her colleagues looked through the window of the door, I waved a knowing 'thankyou I've got this under control' wave and let Brianna let rip.

"I mean, take Marie, she can't stand her fucking husband", I assumed Marie was a friend. "He's been having an affair for about four years, treats his family like shit, drinks like a feckin halibut, red meat, obese, red face, smoking, bookies, flat footed shithouse, why does he get to fucking live when Andrew gets cancer and dies. What's that about?" Brianna threw her hands in the air and looked to the heavens. I was unaware of quite what constituted a 'flat footed shithouse' but vowed to find out and liberally use the term in everyday conversation. Brianna collapsed back into the chair, sighed a heaving sigh, and grabbed chunks of her hair in her fists. She looked up into the roof, took a handful of deep breaths, reflecting on the enormity of the statement she had just made. We sat awhile, me in perplexed silence, Brianna catching her breath.

There was no need for me to say anything at this point, Brianna had tapped into her rage. I sat quietly. From a personal perspective I was also a bit terrified of what might happen if I threw myself in front of this particular emotional locomotive.

"I'm sorry" Brianna said quietly when she'd taken a moment. "I must seem like a right bitch to you".

"Not at all" I said, slightly croaking after a few minutes of silence on my part.

"It's part of the process. Grief is individual, personal, and although there are all sorts of theories about anger and denial and bargaining, the reality is everybody does this differently. I can assure you everything you're feeling is normal".

This was, seemingly, the first thing I'd said all day that hadn't irritated the living shit out of Brianna.

"Thanks" she sighed.

She sat back once again in her chair. I was sensing that although as a practitioner I had been at best bumbling, at least Brianna had had something of a breakthrough. Then I really blew it.

"I'm going to go to the theatre next week", Brianna announced, turning a new conversational leaf. "I'm going alone, I need to get used to it".

At this point I skipped off on a hugely naïve and ill-advised monologue about the joys of going to theatre, cinema and live music alone. This was something I'd done many times, no friends chipping in at inopportune moments, sit or stand where you like, as soon as you get over the initial paranoia it's fine, you get your choice of what you see, if it's rubbish you can leave early, and so on and so forth. Brianna waited until I'd finished.

"That's good for you" she replied quietly, "but it's a bit fucking different when your husband's dead isn't it?"

Touche.

There was no easy way round this. I'd blown it, I wasn't experienced enough to deal with the level of anger that Brianna had, and my personality was clearly irksome to her. Retrospectively I have hoped that Brianna would have seen me for what I was, somebody new to the job, making themselves vulnerable trying to help her, and not some bumbling newbie staggering from disaster to disaster and making everything slightly worse. I made my peace with

Brianna. She needed to know that I knew that this wasn't working.

"Brianna" I said after another lengthy pause. "I'm new to the job and I think there's a lot of complexity to your grief. I was thinking the best thing would be to refer you to an experienced counsellor to help you to learn to live with this." Brianna agreed, thank God. I had thought for a horrible paranoid moment that she had enjoyed the whole process, and she saw it as an emotional Clueso and Kato battle. I was so glad to be wrong.

"Yes please, I think that's what I need".

Pleasantries were exchanged and goodbyes said. I never visited Brianna again. This was a huge learning experience for me. I learned that sometimes you're just not the right fit to support somebody. That's nothing personal, it's just how it is.

I saw Brianna a couple of months later purely by chance. She was polite, seemed well and thanked me for helping her. On reflection, what could I have done differently? There's one answer and one answer only: I could've not been myself. But what sort of intervention would that have been? Textbook, mechanical, and workmanlike. It certainly wouldn't have been therapeutic. I learned a lot about good practice though. First, don't look for solutions when there aren't any. Secondly, don't look for consolation when there is none, thirdly, never ever underestimate the power of just listening. That was all Brianna needed. She didn't need to hear my opinion on going to the theatre alone. She just needed to be heard.

I think that has been the thing I, and many other 'solution focussed' people find difficult. When we're listening to somebody, we are helpless even though we're helping. I've talked at length about showing up being 90% of the job. But here I out-thought myself. All I really needed to do was show up and listen, that was all that was needed. And yet I felt the pull to pipe up with an opinion which wasn't needed, wasn't asked for and didn't help. It is always a worthy reminder that any interruption, whether it is welcome, helpful or otherwise, is still an interruption. For my own professional growth, I internalised matters and, and I recognised that I could have just read my year 7 school report here and saved myself 35 years of professional development: I could have just thought before I spoke, not just about what I was going to say, but whether it was necessary to say anything. So, there we are, another intervention, another unnecessary mistake, but pivotally, another lesson learned. Sorry Brianna.

Chapter Twelve

The bureaucratic challenges of organising temporary housing for domestic abuse victims and how to get men to piss in the toilet for a change.

Summer 2017

"You think you could do any better, be my guest, fuck you, I quit".

I slammed my laptop shut, stood up and stormed out of the stifling hot box room I was having my supervision in. I was, as ever, agitated at working for this local authority. The fact that I had to have supervision in a 40-degree room that was about 6 feet by 6 feet, the windows were painted shut and that we weren't allowed to turn off the heating because that would turn the hot water off too, was mere detail, dusty sugar on the iced bun of my grievances if you will.

I was sick of local authority work. In the interests of my own catharsis, I will document some of the reasons why now:

1. There was always piss on the floor in the gents. I asked for a mop and some bleach but was told 'no' by the Facilities Improvements Strategies Committee (a 15 strong executive cavalcade of fuckwits) who told me that for COSHH reasons that wouldn't work, but, if the stationary budget allowed, they would draft a poster for the wall to be laminated asking people, very politely, not to piss on the floor and, should such pissing on the floor occur, to proceed to clean up said piss. Yes really. The Facilities Improvements Strategies Committee added an item to their agenda about the wording of a poster to ask people to manage their own piss responsibly, and were able to free up some funds from the stationary budget for paper, ink, sticky tac, a laminating pouch and labour to print out a poster telling subsequent lavatarians to manage the results of their reckless penises. Sure enough, the piss issue (The portmanteau lover in my wants to call it a pissue) seemed resolved and standards were noted to improve. It subsequently became clear that the stationary application had not allowed for quite enough sticky tac to keep the poster on the wall for the long haul. And so, the poster fell from the wall, somebody accidentally pissed on it, it got thrown away (one can only assume a cleaning services acquisition form was completed and signed in triplicate to

achieve this end), and so, in the absence of a poster reminding men not to piss on the floor, men started to piss on the floor, and we were, after the all too brief halcyon days of the poster, right back where we started.

2. In one of our team meetings, we were given a presentation by the executive chairman of the Facilities Improvements Strategies Committee about what they actually did. He talked about the challenges of modern facilities management, detailing the process of getting the bins moved from reception to by the bike sheds. I still, several years later, type this and wonder if I imagined it. But I can confirm with no embellishment at all, that there was a display board with a laminated piece of paper that said, 'move the bins from reception to out by the bike sheds' with a big, proud rubber stamp over it sporting the proud boast 'COMPLETED'.

3. At the bottom of the staircase next to the lift there was a sign that said: 'This way to better health and fitness', when you followed the arrow, a second poster said, 'use the stairs not the lift'. Underneath the text it said in quite unforgivable Comic Sans font, 'Promoted by Phil McInally'. Phil McInally had, through his own initiative and ingenuity, designed and put these posters up. Not only

that, he was so proud of his efforts that he wanted everyone to know he had done this and put his name on the poster.

As it transpires Phil McInally was the building's Healthy Choices Champion, an unpaid position for which Phil McInally was the only applicant. Rumour has it he secured the position after a second, very gruelling, interview. This was, however, a perfect role for somebody like Phil McInally, who my grandmother would have described as 'like a postman - all bollocks and bad teeth'. Despite this, Phil McInally was coerced into spending 15 minutes in the company of his line manager (a surly, newly qualified social worker 20 years his junior), at half past four every afternoon to discuss what he had achieved that day. This was part of his 'Performance Management Pathway'. Phil McInally was, very unfortunately, dreadful at his actual job. However, The People Team (the HR Department had been subject to a lengthy period of consultation and rebrand), had stated quite categorically that a member of staff being shit at their job is in no way a justification for their dismissal. Now, I know what you're thinking, if Sisyphean, mythical tasks such as getting people to walk upstairs, moving bins and stopping men from pissing on the floor were the cause of such bureaucratic peacocking, then how in the wide, wide world of sports could we navigate the highly competitive world of stopping vulnerable people from dying of neglect? I'm going to take a big deep breath and make a cup of tea, then prepare my poor laptop for an angry and relentless onslaught. I suggest you do the same, or pour something a little stronger for yourself too. There's a possibility you'll learn some stark truths and perhaps one or two new swear words.

This new referral was handed to me during the scorching hot summer of 2018. Obviously, the office was fraught with news of being unable to either turn the heating off or open the windows. I feel like I've flogged that particular dehydrated horse. I had recently submitted my notice to take my newly qualified skills into hospice care and leave adult services forever. My belief that knowing the end was nigh for me would in some way ease my rage over cost-cutting, bureaucracy, red tape, bullshit and nonsense proved lamentably incorrect. This tale only proved to remind me what a good call it was to be heading out.

I was given the referral of a woman by the name of Karen, a lady with a moderate learning disability. The first name on the referral was the manager of the care provider, the agency who supported Karen in the community to do shopping, access advice, or whatever else was on the support plan. I called the care manager who invited me to the dusty portacabin in the middle of a massive car park that doubled as their office.

"Don't bother paying for parking, we haven't in 4 years, and nobody noticed" I was told. I paid for parking. By this stage in my career, I was just about convinced the universe hated me enough to send a traffic warden on today of all days.

"Morning" beamed Amy jovially, a rural lady in her late 40's who set up her own care agency out of sheer bloody mindedness when her elderly mother was at the end of her life 5 years previous. I liked Amy, she saw me as honest because I didn't buy into local authority bullshit. I also let her know that, yes, above all other lies you're being spun at the moment, the Strengths Based Approach is desirable because it means we can cut an absolute shitload of care packages. My last job in this local authority involved cutting a one hour a week package of support for a 96-year-old blind lady because 'she could shop online'. Needless to say, these were not the sort of changes I was trying to effect in the world. As you can imagine, I wasn't staying 'on message' a lot of the time and harnessed a good reputation with the care providers of the county for gobbing off about the incompetence of senior management whenever the kettle switch was flicked. Amy made coffee and filled me in.

Karen was in her late 40's. She had a son in special education who lived in foster care with regular visits. Her partner, Ivor, was known to be psychologically and financially abusive. She had wanted to leave him for many years. These years had been plagued with stolen money, control, coercion, and regular reminders that Karen was a pointless and useless subhuman who only existed in the magnificent one berth caravan she did due to his generosity. Ivor was a piece of shit (Amy's words, not mine); a chain smoking, alcoholic, domestically abusive, pub bully who came from a long line of chain smoking, alcoholic, domestically abusive pub bullies. Amy explained that Karen had finally made the decision after years of support to finally make a break for it and leave Ivor. Like most vulnerable people who have been abused, she had no clue of her own worth and what could she achieve if she was allowed to try. No sooner had Amy started to talk me through the finer details, Karen walked through the door. She had a supermarket carrier bag ('phone charger, toothbrush, clean pair of knickers') and that was all she had left with apart from her phone and the clothes on her back.

Karen was a tall and, by her own admission, scrawny lady. She wore ripped blue jeans and a baggy, grey woollen sweater. Her skin was ruddy after years of all types of abuse, and her dank greasy blonde hair, complete with a few months of natural dark root growth evidenced a lack of self-care and self-esteem. Karen started the conversation with the charm you would expect from somebody who only knew a life of abuse:

"Fucking hell, you're a bit fat" she began.

"And very nice to meet you too" I said, refusing to look in any way bothered although I really was. I was drinking heavily at this stage in life, and the exhaustion from the hungover commute left me with little time, energy or motivation to exercise. I didn't look good, and I knew it. Karen went on to tell me that after years of having her money stolen and generally being treated as a serf, she had taken Amy's advice and 'run away', an expected term from somebody who had been abused and treated like a child all her adult life. The salient point was that Karen was now homeless and unless somewhere was found quickly to house her, she would either be returning to her caravan of

horrors or sleeping on the street. This was a small, rural market city in Southwest England. Homelessness was not something that garnered any level of sympathy with the residents. Karen needed help and needed it now.

"Ok" I said after hearing the details, *"What are the plans for the rest of the day?"*

Amy told me that Karen would be spending the day at the office, there was a lounge and supplies there so she would be safe and taken care of until I could go back to the office and quickly arrange somewhere for her to stay. I called the housing office, a ten-minute walk away, they said they may be able to help and advised we head straight over there. Karen and I took the short walk saying very little.

The housing office was every bit the Dystopian cesspit Daily Mail readers and Tory politicians feel that the vulnerable deserve. A ticketing system as favoured by Tesco deli in the 80's decided who got seen next. Rows of bright yellow plastic seats, bolted to the floor, rested the weary and hopeless; Young single mums with pushchairs, newly released prisoners, Eastern Europeans eyed with suspicion by the staff and general public alike, wheelchair users, ex-military staff who thought their service would buy freedom from such trauma, people with crutches, every skin colour, every sexuality, every gender, every religion were here trying to climb out of an endless hole. Whilst the housing office carried with it an undercurrent of bigotry and prejudice, every person was treated with equal contempt. Whether it was for coming to this country for a better quality of life, having the audacity to own a phone or have tattoos on your body when you couldn't afford baby formula, or audaciously believing that being homeless in a world of wealth, or hungry in a world full of food just wasn't good enough, all were here, despairing and needing help from those who were reluctant to give it. Karen sat quietly, seemingly untroubled and unsurprised by the scene.

As I lamented the misfortune of those poor lost souls, a man at one of the housing desks who had been getting more and more animated started to pummel the desk in frustration:

"How fucking hard is it? Why can't we just sort it out. I made a fucking mistake. I paid for my fucking mistake, but you people are just going to keep punishing me forever", his voice broke into a cry in his final words.

The man who was in his 60's in an ill-fitting suit with cropped grey hair was quickly accosted by two large security guards, removed from the building and dropped in a heap on the pavement outside. He didn't move. It wasn't that he couldn't move, he just had nowhere to move to. He had no reason to move. I caught a glimpse of his face through the ceiling to floor windows. He lay on the pavement in the foetal position, eyes wide open, staring forward, hopeless. Karen glanced in his direction:

"Boomerang". She said to me.

"What's that Karen?"

"They get out of prison, tries to get housing, when it all kicks off, they get nicked, back in the jail".

This was the problem in a nutshell for so many. So many make mistakes, serve their punishment, but then just aren't afforded the ability to get themselves on the right path. One of many harsh truths I learned that day, was that after a conviction, the straight and narrow isn't always an easy path to get on to. I felt for the man on the pavement. I allowed myself to fashion a narrative of a man who had left prison that day and sworn blind to himself and those who hadn't given up on him that today would be different. Many leave prison with hope and resolution to change, but find bureaucracy stands in the way. Before I could disappear too far down my rabbit hole our number was called, and so began a rather frustrating and dismissive 60 seconds.

Karen and I sat at a desk with a lady who had clearly spent far too long working in public facing roles. I gave a short summary of Karen's life so far but was interrupted:

"She doesn't have the capacity to sign for a tenancy".

"Excuse me?" I replied, taken aback to say the least.

"She doesn't have the mental capacity to understand signing on for a tenancy".

"But... You haven't spoken to her" I replied incredulously, furiously, with absolute disbelief filling me.

To be clear here, the staff member was referring to the Mental Capacity Act (2005). She was suggesting that Karen didn't have the ability to understand, retain, communicate and weigh up the consequences of signing up for a tenancy. And to be fair, she was probably right, but the attitude and dismissive nature of the staff member towards a vulnerable and highly in danger person infuriated me.

"And technically she is homeless by choice" the staff member said, even more dismissively, completely it would seem, ignorant of Karen's plight, in no way admiring of her making the bravest decision of her life.

Karen had spent years being told she needed to leave Ivor by various carers, she had no friends; that it was for the best, that she was worth more and could be more if she left him, that independence would be the making of her, that she may even be able to get and hold down a job and find a nice partner. She might get to live happily ever after. But here she was. In the eyes of the housing office no different to the man in the ill-fitting suit lying on the pavement, a faceless inconvenience without a story.

"Is there anything that can be done? This lady is vulnerable and will be sleeping on the streets tonight if I can't find somewhere for her to go." I pleaded with increasing desperation.

"Sorry" the staff member replied raising her eyebrows and faking a smile.

I could see with the clarity of cold gin how this was going to pan out. And I could see with the same clarity why the man in the ill-fitting suit had got so furious so quickly. There was no care, no compassion, no humanity, just jobsworth, red tape bullshit; ambitionless faces without empathy doing all they could to sweep the vulnerable under the carpet. I was sickened. Karen stood up meekly with neither expression nor emotion when I told her we were wasting our time and needed to go back to the office to think of another plan. We walked in silence through the town. We returned to Amy's office. I updated a wearisome Amy on the situation. My update quickly turned to ranting which then moved as swiftly to swearing. But we had a plan. I was going to complete an emergency urgent care funding application and arrange bed and breakfast accommodation for her. Being an alcoholic social worker, I was privy to the more affordable drinking and staying locations in the town, so all I really needed to do was complete the paperwork and get it signed off.

I hurried back and saw one of the three senior social workers from my team. For purposes of ease, they will be referred to as Senior 1, Senior 2, and Senior 3. Any emergency urgent funding application would have to be signed off by them then agreed by a senior manager then sent to the finance team.

I advised Senior 1 of the situation; told him the only thing I could do was complete an emergency urgent funding application and find Karen a local Bed and Breakfast to stay in. To minimise this from becoming the sort of read that makes you throw your book or device across the room, I will now give a concise, chronological account of how the following few hours went:

12:15 I tell Senior 1 I need to do an emergency urgent to arrange bed and breakfast accommodation for a vulnerable client. He asks if we've been to the housing office. I say we have, and they say the client doesn't have capacity to sign up for a tenancy.

12:32 Paperwork completed and sent to senior 1.

12:47 I go to see Senior 1 and ask him if he's signed it off yet. He says it isn't clear on the paperwork why she needs accommodation. I tell him I made it clear that she has left an abusive partner. He replies that it doesn't say specifically that she will be 'homeless' in the paperwork just that 'she will have to sleep on the streets.'

12:53 Begrudgingly add this detail to paperwork and send to Senior 1.

12:57 It's clear Senior 1 has gone to a meeting for the rest of the day so paperwork is sent to Senior 2. Senior 2 asks if we've been to the housing office. I say we have, and they say the client doesn't have capacity to sign up for a tenancy.

13:15 Senior 2 asks why the client can't just go home. I advise her to read the paperwork fully but frustratedly explain the lady is vulnerable, has a learning disability and has left an abusive partner.

13:55 Senior 2 sends paperwork to senior manager who asks to see me. Senior manager asks if we've been to the housing office. I say we have, and they say the client doesn't have the capacity to sign up for a tenancy.

She also asks why the sentence 'She will be homeless tonight' has been added clumsily to the end of the paperwork. I advise that Senior 1 said that 'she will have to sleep on the streets' was not quite clear enough. We agree that senior 1 is a pedantic buffoon.

Senior manager sends paperwork to Area Manager, who sends to Head of Safeguarding, who sends to Head of Prevention (now there's an ironic job title for a social services executive), all of whom ask the same questions about the housing office, whether she is voluntarily homeless and just generally do whatever can be done to shunt this little problem to somebody else's desk.

15:30 I go to see my manager to ask what's going on. Nothing is going on. Evidently the funding application is on somebody's desk somewhere and nobody is really taking this as seriously as I am.

I go down to the office where I know one or all of these senior managers are sitting (extended lunch breaks, training, sick days and travel time have severely depleted their numbers). I go on a rant that I can only liken to Judith in Monty Python's Life of Brian at the People's Front of Judea. I can remember saying:

"Look, it's perfectly simple. This lady is vulnerable, she is at risk of abuse, she is homeless and sleeping on the streets if we do not do something now".

The Head of Prevention bid me calm down and told me he would be calling the Executive Director to discuss.

"No." I responded, knowingly disabling my career trajectory. *"No more meetings, no more phone calls, no more paperwork. We are failing this person, and we need to deal with it now".*

16:45 Emergency management strategy meeting is called which agrees that the best course of action is an emergency urgent funding application to find a bed and breakfast for Karen.

16:55 I call a local bed and breakfast and book Karen in for two weeks. Just as I'm on the phone, Senior 3 approaches my desk from behind. She's been in meetings all afternoon. She asks why we didn't just go to the housing office.

I count to ten, smile, take a deep breath, look to the ceiling, consider the possible consequences of anything I might say or do, then realise that I am well within my rights to lose my fucking shit.

I spin around on my swivel chair, explain that 2 senior social workers, 1 senior manager and 4 executive managers have taken the best part of five hours, three meetings and around 15 phone calls to draw a conclusion that I was able to draw myself in some 60 excruciating seconds in the housing office. So yes. I had been to the Housing Office and quite frankly, it hadn't ended that fucking well.

After all this nausea all I had to do was let Karen and Amy know it was sorted. I had been keeping Amy in the loop all day, so she knew I was very close to ramming myself in the shredder. Amy put her hand over the phone mouthpiece, turned to Karen and told her accommodation had been arranged and where to go.

"He took his fucking time didn't he?" Karen responded, indifferent to my efforts.

Amy thanked me. She knew what sort of hoops I'd had to jump through that day. She could hear from the exhaustion, frustration and disbelief in my voice that I was at the edge of the edge.

When I think back, my grievances of how this day went are legion, but more than anything else, I think about how the experience was for Karen. I'm glad she didn't know what was going on, unaware that she was an hour or so away from spending the night in a bus shelter or on a park bench. But what did we achieve? Through a culture of cost cutting, risk aversion and a lack of trust in our social workers to make a decision, we achieved the exact same outcome as we would have if they'd just trusted me in the first place. This culture harvested meetings, phone calls, emails, all of which were totally unnecessary, unless the objective was to find a mathematically perfect way of annoying me. This was the ever so frustrating world of adult services. Whether we were walking upstairs, moving the bins, pissing on the floor or ensuring a vulnerable person wasn't sleeping on the street, every job, no matter how simple, was over complicated, over talked, over worked, over thought and over delayed until everybody was certain that their back was covered, and they couldn't possibly get into trouble for not doing their jobs properly. By being risk averse they had created a culture that was exactly what they strived to avoid. For my own mental health, blood pressure and heart it was time to leave.

Chapter Thirteen

Martin

March 2017

I was confused when I received a referral for a sixty year old man called Martian. But after reflection I already had people on my caseload called Death, Jupiter and Venus, so Martian didn't seem too unlikely.

The client was what the referral called an 'ex drug addict'. A man in his late 50's with poor living arrangements, experiencing the health issues that one generally experiences after 30 odd years of not being able to keep a needle out of one's arm. There was some significant lack of clarity about the referral. His housing arrangements, health need and actual care requirements were all unclear. Nobody was able to tell me where the referral had come from, however there was mention of an estranged adult daughter who was next of kin. There was a phone number for 'Martian'.

There had been a clear admin issue that this client had become aware and quickly weary of.

"Martin. M. A. R. T. I. N. I'm not called fucking Martian. My dad didn't hate me *that* much" said Martin, sparking an early psychodynamic field day.

I tried to ask some basic questions, but Martin wasn't keen on talking on the phone. I asked if he was happy to meet somewhere or come to the office.

"No chance, sorry" wheezed Martin helplessly, "Can you come here?".

I agreed I would, I was available that moment so siad I would head straight over to see him. The complexities of the life of an '(ex) drug addict' instantly started to unfold.

"Don't knock the door when you get here", Martin demanded, "call me when you arrive, I'll make it to the window and throw a key down for you ".

"Sure, ok" I replied, already noting the need for a key safe at Martin's flat.

Martin lived on a straight, 800 house long road that went from the City Centre ring road out to the valleys and mountains of the magnificent Welsh border. His flat was nearer to the city than the end of the road and was situated on the 4th floor of a gothic looking Victorian town house in a long row of similar buildings.

I found the house, called Martin, who took several minutes to answer, and then took another minute or so to make it up to the bedroom window, at which point a key on a piece of string landed on the asphalt next to me. Everything about the house was run down; cracked windows, overgrown garden, weeks old bin bags, an old oven and toilet sat by a rickety, long since disused garden shed.

This once magnificent town house was very much a representation of Martin himself. I let myself into the house, shoving the bright red front door with a jolt. What came next was an assault on the senses. Cigarette smoke, cannabis smoke, Heroin smoke, rotten food, dirty clothes, and just general rot. Old post lay unopened with several different names on the floor and in a cardboard box in the corner. There were several once white, now yellowing envelopes scattered about. There was a staircase with a once ornate, but now rickety banister, each step had carpet, the original colour of which was uncertain, but every step had holes worn through the fabric. It was a very long time since anybody had taken care of this house, again, as I would find out, a reflection of Martin's own situation.

There were two ground floor flats, two first floor flats and a kitchen that I can still smell now. Everything was brown.

Old pots and plates were stacked up in the sink overgrown with mould and bins were overflowing. A single glazed cracked window showed a long but overgrown and unkept garden.

The smell from the kitchen was brutal. I noted a full box of eggs with a sell by date many months lapsed and an unopened loaf of Mother's Pride bread that had turned to green sludge. Underfoot was a cocktail of dust, grit and unidentified stickiness that ever so slightly slowed down my walking. I looked up the final flight of stairs and saw a single dark red door standing slightly ajar with a hole that looked like it had been kicked at some point. This was Martin's flat. I pushed the door and called out the expected 'hello'. The flat was small and unpleasant. Martin called me in.

"Hello. Thank you for coming."

Martin was unhealthily thin, lying on a mattress on the floor. He was wearing jeans, white socks and a grey v neck jumper, all of which were several sizes too big, clearly from a time when he was in a better and undoubtedly healthier place. There was an unkempt antique dresser with a cracked mirror, a few CD's, a pile of clean clothes a friend had washed for him, and a very large pile of boxes containing nutrition shakes. Martin half sat, half lay, leaning on his elbow as I introduced myself. Whilst he had no specific diagnosis to speak of, or certainly nothing he was prepared to share with me, he was clearly a very unwell man.

"It's good of you to help me" Martin half-whispered as he tried to sit up. I made myself comfortable on his only other piece of furniture, a short bar stool that he had no doubt liberated from a pub at some point in his chequered past.

"Tell me a bit about yourself Martin."

I like this conversational opener; it's open and gives the person you are supporting the control over what they tell you. Anything that's important comes out early and you're left in little doubt of what matters to that person. I'd only asked Martin to tell me about himself, but he proceeded to give me the most adroit teachings about the world of addiction that I could imagine.

"Well, I'm from London originally. I was a journalist with the Fleet Street pack, mostly News of the World. I was a young reporter when the Wapping move happened and that changed a lot of how things were. It was an exciting time, but it was toxic. You'd get in about half nine, work a couple of hours, pub for lunch about 12:00, sometimes for a couple of hours, sometimes all afternoon. That's where the stories came from. Get down the Prospect of Whitby early doors and by the time you'd sunk a few beers you'd have enough copy to knock out what you needed to for tomorrow's edition".

Martin romanticised about London in the 1980's; the lights of Piccadilly Circus, the clubs, the pubs in the West End, the late nights in Soho getting up to all sorts of debauched behaviour, the casinos, running into well-known footballers on the lash in Strand or Covent Garden. All too soon the ever-excited hedonism of the eighties evolved into narcotics.

"Everybody was on cocaine. You might not remember this but even Frank Bough on breakfast TV got found out snorting Coke to get himself out of his pit in the morning" Martin explained.

"Everything was fair game, everyone in the office was on it, there was piles of it everywhere. The thing about addiction is you never know if you're an addict or not until you stop. And I never had to. Drink, Heroin, Coke, it was cheap, it was in good supply, and everybody did it, in work, after work, on breaks from work. It was what we did".

As with many addicts, the ability to move on with your life as the world changes around you left Martin in trouble. The internet, social media, explosions in the amount of TV channels you could watch turned print journalism from a boy's club with an open-door policy to a vocation that required university qualifications and, if not any actual principles, at the very least a competitive edge and a hard work ethic.

Martin talked up his journalistic credentials and skills, but it was becoming clear that, whilst he was surplus to requirements in eyes of the London tabloid editors and could no longer command the significant salary of 'The Glory Days', he had slipped headlong into addiction, and now he no longer had the means to pay for it. He certainly wasn't part of a working culture that tolerated it. Martin sold his house and found a job as a reporter in a local newspaper in the west of England and relocated, renting a flat on what he convinced himself was a temporary basis.

"Thing with Heroin", Martin began "is that you always work on the basis that you're going to quit tomorrow. Nobody buys much because today is the last day. I won't buy enough for tomorrow because I'll convince myself that tomorrow will be the day where you clean up and change your ways. I convinced myself that by leaving London I would change anyway".

Martin was unaware of the part in the Narcotics Anonymous book where it states that change of location does not constitute recovery, but this really wasn't the time for me to start being a smartarse, so I stayed quiet.

"Addicts are committed and resilient creatures, they'll find Heroin on the moon if you send them there" Martin said, showing analytical knowledge but unawareness of the paradox of his own shortcomings. He'd moved away to escape his addiction but inadvertently taken it with him. Evidently this is a common mistake that addicts make. He didn't take away the addiction, he just took away the contacts.

"So here I am" Martin concluded forlornly.

I asked about the flat he currently had.

"It's a sublet" Martin snapped at me irritably. He explained how he paid cash once a week to a 'contact' who lived in the flat. As an addict, Martin was cautious to use words like 'friend' or 'mate', evidently believing that such relationships would only end in betrayal, deception or violence either with him as the victim or the perpetrator, such was the dog-eat-dog world of addiction. He explained to me that he paid his 'contact', who was himself a using Heroin addict who rented the flat from a landlord who had not been seen or contacted in many years by the residents. There were 6 or 7 people living in the house in the various flats, each one of them an addict either trying to clean up or beyond the hope of trying.

I asked Martin how he got on with his flatmates.

"I don't speak to my co-tenants" responded Martin by way of correction, once again distancing himself from the personal nature of the term. "They're all junkies here."

"Junkies aren't bad people. Addicts no more choose their addiction than a person with Alopecia chooses hair loss. But when you start, like I did, because everybody else is doing it, you soon separate into two groups, those who can stop whenever they want, and those that can't."

"And I suppose the people that live here are all from the latter group" I suggested in a rare interjection. Martin snorted by way of confirming my suggestion.

"I can remember being at University" Martin segued, "I went in what I suppose they'd call 'Freshers Week' now. The first week was piss up after fuck after club after party" said Martin, making what he clearly remembered as an exotic and sophisticated existence sound rather bleak.

"One or two dropped off in the second week because they wanted to study, then a few more, then maybe one or two stragglers got a warning letter for non-attendance, then before you know it, you're the last man standing, and everyone has settled down and got to work. Well, that is exactly what addiction is like. London was a breath of fresh air, the party started up again this time in the pubs of London with hacks and hangers on. Then suddenly, the job has gone, the party is over, your family have fucked you off. You don't have friends anymore; you have contacts and witnesses to your existence. You can't trust anybody and by fucking God, nobody trusts you."

"Why would nobody trust you?"

Martin sighed, clearly frustrated by the interruption.

"Junkies are simple creatures; they want one thing: drugs" Martin began. "You hear stories of people who steal their granny's savings or smash their kid's piggy banks to get a hit, right?".

I nodded, transfixed. This was quickly becoming a lecture that I could ill afford to miss, for professional reasons or macabre fascination.

"Well, those people aren't fucking evil, are they?" Martin was getting into his stride now; I was on his territory, and he was clearly warming to my interest.

"No junkie wakes up in the morning hoping to fuck over a family member or hurt somebody who loves them. It's just the addiction doesn't offer a choice. When a junkie is sick with withdrawal and they need, and I mean medically fucking need a hit, they see the world in a binary way, things that well either help or hinder the procuring of Heroin. People who have never been addicted to anything take this shit so fucking personally. That's why there's nothing worth stealing in this flat, every other flat will be the same. Every single person here has ransacked every other person's flat at one time or another. The only reason the toaster and microwave haven't been nicked and sold is that none of these pondlife cunts could be bothered to clean them up". I wanted to laugh, the venom and swift delivery of the final line was comical, but I got the impression that Martin wouldn't appreciate the compliment.

So here Martin was, in a house share with other lost souls stretching on the rack of their own decision making and subsequent addictions. He had a small pension from his time working on the newspapers, but this covered very little. He had taken a lump sum early which he spent on a drug binge that lasted some two months, and now, without a registered address he couldn't claim benefits, his poor lung capacity from years of smoking various substances had left him unable to walk even to a local shop, so he depended on Mike, his only friend, to buy food, collect prescriptions and generally keep him alive. There was little doubt Martin needed help, but as was consistent through his life, he wasn't prepared to make decisions that were in his best interests. We talked about arranging a package of care.

"Not here" Martin replied, once again his manner was impatient and snappy. "I don't want carers seeing me here. And anyway, I can't be doing with getting up to throw the key down".

"Would you consider moving?" I asked, fearing an angered response.

"How the fuck would that work?".

By this stage I was weary of Martin's inability to think positively about anything. My inner monologue snapped back "Don't have a go at me mate, I never asked you to take fucking Heroin". Of course, I restrained myself and opted for something a little more diplomatic and professional.

"Well," I began carefully, *"You're subletting a flat that isn't really fit for purpose or safe, but you have no contract or details of your landlord, so I'd suggest that technically that constitutes you being homeless".*

Martin looked animated for the first time since I arrived.

"I could do an application for emergency housing then we could put a package of care in place to ensure all your needs are met".

Martin then proceeded to deliver a list of requirements:

"No nursing homes, no sheltered accommodation, I don't want anything on the south side of town either".

"You're welcome, Martin", the inner monologue piped up before being stifled by reality.

When people find out what I do and say, 'oh that must be very rewarding', I always regale them of tales of clients who issue their demands that they would like me to meet before they allow me the privilege of helping them. One would be forgiven for thinking that an unhealthily underweight man living in squalid and filthy conditions, with, and I had only just noticed this, a half full bucket of his own dark coloured urine next to his mattress, who was unable to source even the most basic provisions for himself, would be perhaps a little more grateful and a little less choosy. Life in social work has taught me that this is often not the case and Martin was living proof.

I agreed with Martin that I would attempt to source some sheltered accommodation provision and investigate how we could support him to move safely. Maybe his standards were low due to years associating with exclusively addicts, maybe Martin was fundamentally just an unpleasant person. Maybe, like many addicts, he lacked the ability to think of himself as worthy of having somebody care about him. In spite of his manner and him representing much that I found objectionable, I cared about Martin, and I wanted to help him. I gave my farewells and told Martin I would be back to visit and would start work on finding accommodation for him. The first step was to see how to start arranging the appropriate benefits he was entitled to. His GP was able to offer repeat prescriptions of medication and meal replacement shakes, but she hadn't seen Martin in a very long time during which I would think his condition had declined considerably. As a result, it was unlikely that social services and the GP had a sound understanding of his situation.

I made calls to the GP and a local care provider, both of whom were immensely helpful. The GP would arrange to visit Martin at home, and the care provider was able to offer a flat in a supported living complex in the coming weeks. It was all coming together. I could see a future for Martin, even if he was struggling to see one for himself. I hoped somehow that having somebody who was genuinely enthusiastic about helping him to improve his life might rub off on him, maybe he'd start taking care of himself a little. As naïve as it sounds, I wanted this to work. I pictured Martin healthy and happy in his new flat, making friends with other residents, finding things to fill his time that were constructive. I was certain that with the right approach, the right enthusiasm and the right level of care and consideration I could show Martin that life was worth living and worth living well. I text Martin to let him know how it was going and received a favourable response.

"That all sounds great. Thankyou. Martian".

I sincerely hoped this was an attempt at humour and not a typo but replied with a 'you're welcome'. We weren't at the emoji stage of our relationship, if such a thing existed, so he'd just have to hope I understood and enjoyed the joke.

Then the phone rang, I looked at my mobile and saw an unrecognised number. I replied.

"Hi, is that Andy?" said a youthful sounding Yorkshire accent on the other end of the line.

"Yes, hello, what can I do for you?"

"I'm Hayley. I understand you've been supporting my father, Martin".

"Hi Hayley" I replied, *"I'm really sorry but I can't discuss clients over the phone without consent from them".*

"That's fine, I get it" replied Hayley "I'm just glad he's getting help. We haven't spoken in over five years".

"Oh, I'm sorry to hear that" I replied with genuine remorse.

"Oh, it's fine" said Hayley, "He was never there growing up, we knew he existed and he'd occasionally pop by to remind us he was alive and pretend he cared about us, but for the most part he's never been much of father. Not much of a man at all".

Hayley's gentle northern accent sounded warm and affectionate, to hear her communicating such hurt and, worse than disliking her father, she felt nothing for him, sounded so oddly paradoxical. A warm voice communicating the coldest of messages.

"Some of my family worry, he's still in occasional contact with my mum, so I just wanted to say thank you for looking out for him. He's such a pathetic little man so I'm glad somebody is doing something to help". Hayley talked exactly like the binary obstacle to addiction that Martin had talked about earlier. Here was the daughter of an addict. There was nothing she could do to help him get his fix, so she was therefore no use to him. He was a neglectful father and now she had nothing to feel for him or his welfare. Hayley seemed like a compassionate and likeable soul. I could totally understand why she felt like she did. She communicated indifference but betrayed that emotion by calling to thank me and to check on his welfare. After a lifetime of hurt, rejection and disappointment, Hayley still had it in her heart to make a call and show that she loved her dad, albeit from a distance.

I was buoyed by this, even more convinced that a healthy and productive life awaited Martin if he could stay away from Heroin, the wrong people, and get on a positive path. Now there was even evidence of a compassionate family, or at the very least, a family that could become compassionate again with the right approach and the right love. Everything appeared to be going in a good direction, the placement paperwork was completed and approved as quickly as one could expect, Martin let me access details of various corners of his past to ensure all applications were made quickly and approved without obstacle. This was becoming a social work intervention that I was going to be proud of, a bar raising, textbook definition of how to work with addicts. Martin was going to live well, healthily and long. It was going to be ok. Then Martin died. Unexpectedly, without fuss, panic or distress, he just died on his mattress in his sleep.

The call came from the safeguarding team. The police had raided the house on intelligence about stolen goods and movement of Heroin, cocaine and crystal meth. During the raid, the police had gone to the top floor, found Martin's front door open and found him dead. I thanked the safeguarding officer for letting me know and hung up the phone. I was sat on a pod of five social workers and a senior and told the team.

"Martin Draper has died".

"Bloody hell mate" Replied my senior with disbelief, "The work you put in there, you must be gutted".

I hadn't even reflected on the waste of work, just the waste of life. I'd arrived in Martin's life too late. I sat a while staring at my computer screen then decided to check Martin's record; sure enough there it was, highlighted with an alert 'New information- check record', I clicked the link and saw the ostensibly callous wording 'client dead'.

I was shaken by the news. For whatever reason some deaths affect you more than others, and Martin affected me, not because as was the case on other occasions, I was particularly affectionate or drawn to Martin, he had little I could relate to, but it was the overwhelming sorrow that we didn't get the positive outcome, the uplifting conclusion, the 'happily ever after'. As I pondered, reflected and pretended I wasn't experiencing any emotional impact and tapped away randomly at my keyboard, my phone rang. It was Hayley. The challenge here was that I wasn't sure if Hayley knew that her dad was dead. Offering condolences from the off could constitute a weapons grade faux pas, so I treaded with caution.

"Hayley," I began, *"How are you?"*.

Hayley was clearly crying; she took deep breaths every few words to make herself understood.

"You know he's dead, don't you?" she asked.

"I just heard. I'm so sorry".

The conversation was short, Hayley wanted to make sure I knew, her family had been alerted as next of kin by the police. A saving grace was that there was no suggestion of foul play, but it being a sudden death and in the circumstances of his living arrangements, Hayley would have to travel from Yorkshire to identify Martin's body.

"I tried to explain I hadn't spoken to him in about five years, I haven't seen him in nearly ten, I'm trying not to think about what state he will be in" Hayley sighed.

I tried to understand the mindset that Hayley would be in, and it occurred to me what many people I have supported in the past have told me about the death of an estranged or distant family member. Hayley wasn't just grieving the death of Martin; she was grieving the relationship she never had with him. All the time he was alive she had hoped that he would overcome his addiction and attempt to make things right, apologise, offer consolation for his wrongs, or just do something that told her he was sorry for the way he had been. Martin never chose his addiction, we know this. Many people see addiction as a choice. The reality is that Martin treated his family badly through no fault of their own, but through it all, the addiction, the lies, the disappointment, Hayley still had hope for her dad. Her compassion and love for him had long since departed, but news of his death brought the demise of the hope she had for him. She explained all of this to me, the torment, remorse and conflict within her overshadowing every word. She still craved a relationship with a man who had disappointed and lied at every opportunity.

I had lost nothing in comparison and felt mildly infuriated by my colleagues' comments about the amount of work I had wasted. To me it wasn't a waste, I hadn't succeeded in 'saving' Martin, but Hayley had hope for him, and knowing that I had valued him, validated him and saw his potential worth as a person was a source of comfort to her.

Hayley must have thanked me about ten times during the conversation. It was humbling to me that somebody so bereft, experiencing such a diverse and conflicting range of emotions was still able to be grateful. Through it all, the experience of the flat, the story Martin told, the unexpected, comfortable but ultimately undignified death, the aftermath, through all of that, the word Hayley used more than anything else was 'thankyou'.

I ended the call and advised my colleagues I was taking a break. Of all the negatives and disappointment, I would never forget the lessons that Martin taught me about addiction, and what Hayley taught me about hope.

Chapter Fourteen

Enid, Darren and a love letter to Dowlais

June 2016

During my time working in the West of England I was handed the most curious of referrals. A 40-year-old man by the name of Darren had, to all intent and purpose, gone missing. A brief look through the records showed that this was in fact, not quite the case.

Darren had a physical disability, Cerebral Palsy, but was neurotypical. In the absence of any family in the town, he spent his weekends in Dowlais visiting his elderly aunt and uncle. On one such visit, Enid's husband Dai had died suddenly of a heart attack. It was a quiet Sunday afternoon, the roast beef eaten, cleared away and washed up. Dai sat, with his newspaper and pipe, fell asleep and never woke up again. He was 85. Darren, who relied on Dai for lifts to and from his home some 40 miles away, had just never gone home. Fourteen months had now lapsed, during which Darren had had no formal package of care, no GP appointments, in fact very little to evidence that he even existed anymore.

Dowlais was a small village in Merthyr Tydfil, South Wales. It had traditionally been a community that provided workers for the steel and iron works, but, like many south Wales communities, the industries had fallen foul of poor economic conditions, imports and generally being held in little esteem by central government. Over the following years the population had gradually moved away leaving around 6,000 souls. Such factors did nothing to tell me the true stories of this community.

I called the phone number I had been given for Enid. She answered the phone in age old tradition 'good morning, Dowlais 355492'. Her voice, aged though it was, spoke with the lilting South Wales accent that poetry and song was written for. I introduced myself, saying I was a social worker and was just checking in to see how Darren was doing.

"Oh, he's fine, we get by you know", she replied.

"May I speak with him?" I asked.

"Well not really, he's ever so crippled he is and doesn't do so well with the phone, and any way, still grieving we are, since Dai died".

It didn't seem right to me that somebody would grieve for fourteen months, but if my experience had taught me one thing, it's that grief doesn't have rules or boundaries. It most certainly doesn't adhere to timelines. After some conversational toing and froing, Enid agreed to let me visit Darren with a resigned, but ever so warm "well you're very welcome to visit us, but we're managing fine, and we really don't need anything". I made an appointment for the following week and thanked Enid for her time.

The day came, I left in the early morning and headed off towards Dowlais. The drive was uneventful but the scenery breath-taking. New dual carriageways careered through valleys, hills and mountains. After life in the West of England, the absence of very many people was noticeable. My sat nav brought me into Dowlais. Rows of terraced dark grey, light grey, cream and light blue houses stretched out down the road to the bottom of the village. Above the houses, the hills and mountains were lit up with unseasonal sunshine. The February wind whistled through the streets creating a bitter breeze. Every house had neat blue and black boxes of tin cans and plastic bottles awaiting collection.

I found Enid's address and parked my car. Every house seemed to have lacy net curtains providing a wave of twitches as I walked to her house. I rang the doorbell. I could make out a short image walking slowly towards the door through the frosted glass. The door opened and there was Enid. An immaculately dressed lady in her 80's in a floral dress and cardigan. Her grey hair was tightly pulled back, and she wore little wire glasses that circled her eyes.

"Bore Da" I said with a pronounced English accent "I'm Andy, we spoke on the phone".

"It's pronounced Borrer Da" Enid said with a smile, "but that was a lovely attempt, thank you".

Enid's house exuded warmth and comfort.

"Go on through" she pointed to the lounge, as I walked through the hallway, I glanced right into what Enid called the 'Sunday Room'; it was an immaculately kept dining room with thick patterned carpet, framed photos of family on the wall, a dining table, six chairs and an imposing wooden bookcase, the top part of which was a glass display cabinet holding trinkets and war medals from the second world war. There was not a speck of dust in sight. I continued my short walk to the living room. An electric fire glowed in front of a tiled fireplace, modestly papered walls, family pictures, horseshoes, a few display teapots, many ornaments that were in practice love letters to Wales, and a fading tapestry in a glass frame that said:

"Life is going to work.

To dig a hole,

To earn the money,

To buy the food,

To get the strength,

To go to work,

To dig a hole".

I'm guessing there is some monotony suggested here, perhaps pathos, but all I saw was charm. As traditional as this home was, there was no anachronism. Welsh pride exuded through every pore of this community.

Enid invited me to sit down. The wooden legged furniture with soft arms and white lace protectors lying over the top provided perfect comfort. Darren sat in the corner. He was dressed smartly in plain trousers, a collared shirt and red v necked jumper.

"He wanted to make an effort because we had a guest" said Enid proudly. Darren sat, his arms and legs jerked slightly as he said hello and thank you for coming. His speech was slurred and a little slow, but patience proved the virtue and provided all that was needed to understand Darren. I asked how they were coping.

"Oh, we do fine" replied Enid warmly.

"We do fine thank you" Darren said echoing the sentiment. During the visit, four separate neighbours telephoned to ensure Enid and Darren were ok.

"The neighbours help whenever we need them to, that's how we are here. We're like a big family, see? Everyone looks out for everyone else."

Enid quickly started talking about the Six Nations Rugby match against England the coming weekend.

"We're ever so excited" she beamed.

"We loves the rugby; the boys are definitely going to win it this year". I pictured a Saturday in Dowlais, the pubs and houses all united in community behind the Welsh rugby team as this whole street was united behind Enid and Darren.

My concerns, however, were correct, Enid explained to me over an immaculately presented pot of tea, complete with matching cup of saucer and vast array of biscuits, that there was no package of care, no occupational health, no physio, no regular care at all. Enid, in her 80's and standing at a fraction above five feet tall was washing, showering, changing, helping to the toilet and doing bedtime routines for Darren all on her own. Occasionally it got too much and she'd maybe ring Bette and Dai next door (there were men called Dai in no less than 5 of the surrounding houses so surnames were used in all communications to avoid confusion). All of the neighbours were happy to help. It occurred to me that while the government had neglected this resilient and proud corner of Wales (they had been left with little investment, few opportunities for the younger population, and very little agency of their own), one thing they did have was a sense of belonging, community and unity that most parts of the country had lost in pursuit of status, wealth and careers. Generations of families united to help each other out and support each other when nobody else would. They were inspiring people, but an absolute nightmare for a social worker. I asked to hear more from Enid about their family history.

"Well, my Dai's been gone some 14 months this week" she said matter of factly. "Steel worker his whole life he was. But truth be told, a lot of him never came back from Aberfan".

The mention of the word 'Aberfan' was followed by a deserving silence. On 21st October 1966, about 6 miles away, 144 people, mostly children at Pantglass Junior School, died when a colliery spoil tip collapsed. The resulting avalanche destroyed the local school and a number of houses. The community had never recovered and didn't expect to. Everyone in the village, and most people in the surrounding communities had a family member or friend killed. The surviving children talked of guilt when they played, worked or even smiled. No disaster has ruptured and broken a British community like it since.

Enid talked of how, when word came through of the disaster in Aberfan, every Iron worker, steel worker, coal miner, farmer and labourer, downed tools and went to help with the search and rescue effort. Enid knew Dai had gone, he was gone for days, sleeping on a church floor, fed by the surviving tortured and bereft community, and digging in his waking hours.

"He never talked about what he saw or what he found" Enid talked in hushed tones.

"But he was never quite the same after that. But we never had children. He didn't want them after that. I'm not sure if he'd feel guilty for having children when others had lost theirs, or if he just couldn't stand the idea of putting himself through the pain that he'd seen others go through that day. But that was his decision. But it turned out well, when Darren was born, we were as good as mam and dad for him anyway". Darren smiled a huge grin when Enid said this, but a tear was visibly streaming down his face.

The victims of Aberfan weren't just those that died. They were people like Dai, forever traumatised, riddled with unnecessary and disenfranchised guilt. This community would never forget and would never want to. The overwhelming sense of heartbreak, loss and trauma lived on and showed little signs of ever going away.

We talked a little more, with Enid and Darren both making perfectly clear that no help was needed, be it practical or financial. The community would step up so no formal intervention was needed. This community had been let down enough, and now it united to help those who needed it without fuss or complaint. It was a breath-taking prospect.

I thanked Enid and Darren for their time and hospitality and finally managed to get them to take a business card from me, promising that if it ever got too much, or they couldn't cope any more, that they would give me a call. Enid promised and shook my hand thanking me sincerely as she led me out into the bitter wind that howled through the valleys. I knew I would never hear from them, and, as frustrated as I was as a social worker, I was inspired by the dogged and industrial determination that held this community together. They were proud, hardworking folk, from a community that embraced and lived its traditions, in this case, pulling together and needing nobody else.

That weekend Wales lost their match to England 16-21 in Cardiff. I very much doubt Enid and Darren let it spoil their day, they really weren't at home to self-pity.

Chapter Fifteen

"Bill Tidy told me to Fuck Off".

September 2003

In 2003, I was working in what can only be described as a mixed bag sheltered living complex. The charity that ran it was generally associated with people with acquired brain injuries, but across the twenty flats were clients with Cerebral Palsy, mental health issues and physical disabilities as well. It was a beautiful community. Most of the people there got on extremely well, shared dark senses of humour, and generally went about their business with aplomb. Martyn was one such character. He was diagnosed with Multiple Sclerosis at the age of 39, now, aged 46 he lived independently with occasional carer input and his young daughter came for regular sleep overs.

Martyn was great fun, standing at little over 5"4 he had a pot belly and a bald head and steel rim glasses. Since his Multiple Sclerosis had escalated, he had developed a Carpe Diem approach to absolutely everything. At the age of 46 he had had his first ever ear piercing, started smoking again twenty years after quitting and even got a tattoo of the legend 'your name' on his left buttock. He was going to get 'free hugs' tattooed on his knuckles but his elderly mother,

Margaret, stepped in at this point. Any time he got drunk, slipped over, forgot to pay a bill, said something inappropriate or swear in front of his daughter and got an angry call off his ex-wife, he had one response:

"It's the MS."

Martyn also had a zinger of a claim to fame: "Bill Tidy once told me to fuck off".

As claims to fame go, the title really did what it said on the tin, but all the same I was keen to get some qualifying information. It transpired Martyn had once been steaming drunk at a church fete. A local cider merchant had a very popular stall that Martyn was keen to patronise and patronise he did. By the time Martyn and his friends had bought and drank far more cider than the merchant had expected to sell, a rather curmudgeonly and irritable TV cartoonist turned up late to the fete as guest of honour, seemingly voicing some disappointment to his agent that such an event wasn't really going to enhance his celebrity status and credibility. Martyn was, by his own admission, in an 'advanced state of refreshment' and commandeered the said TV cartoonist in the interests of getting his autograph. As we know, Bill Tidy was not forthcoming with the goods and requested Martyn take his leave. Martyn being Martyn however, laughed it off stating that "Being told to fuck off by Bill Tidy is a much better story than one where I just got his autograph and lost it". Faultless logic from Martyn as ever. Martyn lived by his own rules and nobody else's, but, by God did he, and all of us, fear his mother.

On this occasion Martyn was going to his GP for his wellness check. I had happily volunteered to give him a lift, at which point he announced that his mother was joining him to "keep things untoward and make sure I don't say anything silly". Martyn's mum was at his flat when I arrived to pick him up. She was the classic Marks and Spencer's, maybe even Waitrose, grandma. To save my descriptive abilities for later on, just Google Mrs Roberts from Fawlty Towers and you'll get a perfect idea of both her appearance and attitude towards working class folk like me.

"Ah. About time" said Margaret abruptly with perfect received pronunciation.

"Sorry Margaret, I thought we said ten o'clock" I said, knowing full well we had said ten o'clock.

"Mrs Hall to you, thank you" replied Margaret bluntly whilst folding and tidying things that really didn't need folding or tidying.

I hoped for a quick meeting with the doctor so I could go about my day. The chaos of Martyn versus the dominant Matriarch of his mother provided a cultural 'unstoppable force versus the immovable object' which suggested to me that this really wasn't going to go well. We took the short drive to the GP surgery which meant Margaret would have to get in the back of my very battered old Ford Fiesta and, much to her chagrin, suffer the indignity of climbing over the folded forward driver's seat as there were no back doors. As Margaret muttered very much over her breath about the inconvenience of the situation, I reflected to her that it was unfortunate that support worker roles really didn't pay enough to buy an expensive car and that the charity sector really couldn't afford anything similar either, so, unless she wanted to shoe-horn herself out of the back of the Fiesta and totter on her heals to the surgery, this was the best option we had.

At the GP surgery Margaret's moaning turned to low level racism. She simultaneously complained about immigrants claiming benefits but also working in reception at the surgery. I got the distinct impression Margaret was not open to any kind of intellectual challenge on this, so kept quiet but raised my eyebrows and shook my head when she said something dreadful. Martyn, who was showing far greater acumen and experience in this area than me, had wisely kept his mouth shut for the duration. The GP however was not quite as prepared to keep his opinions to himself, and he clearly wasn't as intimidated by Margaret as we were either. The appointment began inoffensively enough with relatively polite introductions. The GP was a young man, maybe late twenties, ruggedly handsome in a sort of young Brad Pitt with very little sleep mould. He hadn't shaved for a few days; his tie was undone, and he really wasn't going to be taking any shit.

"Now", Margaret began "My biggest worry is that after many years off cigarettes, Martyn has started smoking again".

The GP gazed at the notes in front of him, casually eyeing up a computer screen simultaneously, without looking up asked:

"How many are you smoking Martyn?"

"About ten a day." Martyn replied sheepishly.

"Ten too many" Margaret interjected at the request of nobody.

"Normal cigarettes, not cigars or cannabis?", he asked, clearly turning the 'nonchalometer' up to eleven in a bid to dampen Margaret's authority.

"Yep, Bensons" Martyn replied.

"Well, I wouldn't worry" replied the GP, turning his swivel chair and smiling directly at Martyn, purposefully ignoring Margaret:

"The MS will kill you a long time before the fags do".

Margaret was displeased. In fact, she looked like she might explode. The thing about being permanently narky and obnoxious is you really don't have anywhere to go when somebody really, properly says something that antagonises you.

"I hardly think…." Began Margaret, losing the use of vocabulary.

"I am Martin's GP, I know him well, I know his health situation well. If you ask for my considered opinion you will receive it" said the GP, in a calm, measured, looking-at-the-notes-again kind of way. He had my admiration. This was compassion. Granted it was dressed up as arrogance with good intention. But it struck me that the GP was prepared to 'take one for the team' to make sure Martyn knew the truth. Then Margaret pressed the red button, in more ways than one.

"He's got piles too. Tell him about your piles" demanded Margaret.

I correctly anticipated that this probably would challenge the realms and boundaries of my professionalism. The GP sighed "Do you want me to have a look?" he asked. I would speculate the votes being 3:1 against at this point but Martyn reluctantly agreed, and they disappeared behind a white curtain as Martyn assumed the position and took off what he needed to.

Rather awkwardly, Margaret and I sat in silence facing the privacy curtain where we could clearly make out the silhouette of Martyn in an uncompromising position, and the GP preparing to shove a finger up his anus.

"If this feels uncomfortable let me know and I'll stop" said the GP clinically.

"I'm not going to fall for a line like that again Doc" replied Martyn immediately.

Margaret shot to her feet and screeched "Martyn" in as shocked and appalled a pitch as her wrinkly throat would allow. There was absolute silence behind the curtain, although the silhouette clearly depicted Martyn with his head buried in the couch stifling guffaws. The GP had withdrawn his index finger from Martyn's anus and was doubled over a plastic chair trying not to laugh.

I sat next to Margaret, my lips clasped together, tears running down my clearly deep red face. It had become all too much as, without even an attempt at an excuse, I broke for cover and staggered into the corridor, took breaths and composed myself. As I walked back into the doctor's office, I could see the examination was now at an end. Martyn and the GP were doing a reasonable job of pretending nothing untoward had happened. Margaret scowled at me with thin lips and razor-sharp gaze. I was in trouble.

After the appointment we drove back to Martyn's flat in silence. As I supported him back into the flat, Margaret told me where Martyn liked to sit. Martyn was able to tell me this himself, and besides, I knew already, but I saw no purpose in letting Margaret know this. I ensured Martyn had no further support needs for the day and took my leave.

Margaret had once again busied herself folding and polishing. On second glance I could see a single tear running down her cheek, she called my name as I was on my way out:

"Thank you, Andrew, it was nice to see you today. Martyn's condition breaks my heart, but it gives me such peace to know somebody like you is taking care of him". I smiled, thanked Margaret and left. I had misunderstood her, and totally overlooked how it might feel to have your only son living with a condition that was gradually taking his independence, movement and eventually his ability to communicate. Margaret was breaking inside and didn't know any other way of managing the situation than by trying to take control, but there was no control to be taken here. She could lead a GP appointment and ensure everybody behaved, but the thing she really wanted to control was the one thing she couldn't. In a heartbeat she stopped being a fearsome force of elderly nature and became a mother who was lost, grieving for the son who was gradually disintegrating in front of her, slowly but progressively and inevitably.

I saw Margaret again a few weeks later and she was back to her hostile and surly self, complaining, patronising and nagging both Martyn and his care staff. Now I understood. She was masking her vulnerability and, it must be said, masking it well. The one occasion she had allowed the mask to slip helped me to see Margaret in a light of compassion and love. Despite her manner which was misguided, I held a great fondness for Margaret, sorry, Mrs Hall.

Both Martyn and his mum lived well in the years that followed. Martyn retained his enthusiasm for life, laughs and mischief whilst Margaret revelled in treating him like a naughty child and generally bossing him and his carers about. They died in the same year, forces of nature, love and unlikely companionship. I remained fond of them both and grateful that they did not spend long apart.

Chapter Sixteen

Robert and Maureen

October 2019

Sometimes hospice work is relentless, it deals you blow after blow. Then when you feel like your day couldn't possibly get any worse it deals you the haymaker right hook that sends you falling to the canvas.

Sometimes though, it introduces you to people who display a level of courage and positivity that makes you absolutely refuse to be beaten. Robert was one such man. He was referred to the Men's Group at the hospice during the height of the Covid pandemic. Robert taught himself how to use the technology to access the group over Zoom and, as became a theme with his life, with claws in and bare teeth grit, got on with whatever the day threw at him.

When Robert first popped up on the screen, he quickly decided the group wasn't for him, keen to spare my feelings, he told me it 'wasn't the right time for me' to join the group. I hear this a lot, routinely from people who I will never see again, but sure enough, a couple of months later he got in touch and said he was ready to make friends and share stories.

Robert fascinated the group and kept them quiet with stories of his travels around the world, his rugby career and his always sensible outlook on the farcical British political landscape. He also had a huge list of co-morbidities, two types of Cancer and Motor Neurone Disease, yet it bore no impact on his outlook on life. Robert's wife often made an appearance on screen too, smiling and gracious. Love emanated through the screen, ever strong after over fifty years together. Everything about Robert and Maureen made you want to work harder, do better and be more, they were just those people, inspiring, positive and incredibly likeable.

As the world returned to its new normal, the group returned to face-to-face meetings. This meant meeting a number of people who knew each other well, face-to-face, for the first time. Robert's physical presence was significant but unimposing. He stood at around six foot five inches tall with curly grey hair, fading age old military tattoos and a thin frame evidencing the unforgiving and ravaging impact of his Motor Neurone Disease.

I can confess to feeling low that day. The Covid pandemic had dished out more than its share of trauma and deaths of people I supported and cared about. It had also prevented our team from working in a professionally intimate way. The raw emotion of handing over the belongings of a patient who had died on the ward to their families was now gone, we now had to the pass over full binbags in a car park whilst dressed in full PPE. Condolences were offered over the phone, not in person. The connections that made the job rewarding for us and made a traumatic time tolerable for our patients and their families were impacted catastrophically. The isolation, fear and derangement of routines left me feeling empty and depressed.

To be clear, it's never effective to tell somebody to 'man up' or 'get over it'. However, sometimes somebody heroic will say something that lifts you up. Today was that day, and that person was Robert.

The group sat chatting; I would generally go around the room asking everyone about how they were. Some would discuss disease, some would touch on it, some would never even let on that they were unwell.

I asked Robert how he was.

"Well, the good news is I'm alive." Robert began.

"Today has been a good day. The battle for me isn't with the disease, it's with myself. If I can find the positives, the wins, it makes my day so much better. Like today, I've done my own shoelaces up. That wouldn't mean anything to most people, but to me it's a huge win. I have another day under my belt where I've just managed to cling on to that one crumb of independence. It means the world. And my family see me doing my best, working hard, getting results. It's so good for them to see that I'm not beaten, especially my grandchildren".

I reflected on my own situation and realised it was beyond my control, but the way I thought about things and acted were very much in my own power.

"Every day I wake up and think 'Yes! Another morning'." Robert continued, this was the first time I'd ever seen this group just sit and listen without quipping, interrupting or questioning. They were transfixed, and I was changed.

"I'm grateful to be here, I'm grateful for all of you, I tied my shoes, brushed my teeth, I'm amongst friends. I know my time is fast coming to an end, but one thing the situation gives you is perspective. I'm not afraid and I enjoy every day for the gift that it is".

Silence, then a ripple of applause from all the men in the room. Robert was, without a doubt the most unfortunate man in the room yet he had seen fit to bless us with his positivity. I honestly felt like he had picked me up and carried me on his shoulders. Happiness really was all about perspective for Robert, his courage was truly remarkable. On behalf of the group, I thanked Robert for his words. You could get a sense of reflection from the men sat on armchairs in a big circle. Many of the men were living with illnesses that would kill them, but none were visibly coming to the end of life as quickly as Robert was.

As the weeks passed Robert's appearance changed. He started to wear a neck brace to prevent his head from tilting, an arm brace to support his grip, and weight fell from his already slim frame. His enthusiasm for life and positivity were, however, completely undented. No man could feel self-pity when Robert was in the room. As the weeks went by Robert even produced a children's book he had written to be sold to raise funds for hospice care. Typically, he wanted to give thanks for something that he had made a most gracious and valued contribution to already. Many of the men in the group were, as ever, buoyed by Robert's spirit and attitude. One of the most beautifully touching things I had seen in a long while is when one of Robert's fellow patients brought his grandson to the session to meet Robert and get his book signed.

Robert was typically humble and quite flabbergasted by the admiration.

As the weeks went by Robert's condition progressed. By this stage the group would meet in person one week and online the next and Robert's appearances both on screen and in person became fewer and further between. I kept in touch, one morning I called Maureen and offered to visit Robert at home, Maureen was grateful for this, telling me that Robert was finding it harder to breathe, eat and speak. I travelled out to the picturesque west country village they had called home for the last forty years.

Robert and Maureen's house was everything you'd expect, immaculate, clean cream carpets, fresh flowers in a vase, pictures of children and grandchildren on wedding days, at graduation, and generally living their best lives. Everything about their home reflected the love, joy and contentment they had enjoyed since getting married fifty years ago. A gracious welcome was given, and I was led into the lounge where Robert was sitting, his oxygen machine nearby. Robert was delighted to see me, making himself breathless with an enthusiastic seated welcome. We briefly chatted and Maureen came in with tea and possibly the finest lemon drizzle cake I have ever tasted (there is stiff competition for this accolade by the way).

Robert wasn't well, he had been suffering from an infection for a few days which took his appetite, as a result he had lost a significant amount of weight that he could ill-afford to lose. His conversation was interspersed with heavy coughs.

Maureen was delightful and incredibly positive, allowing Robert time to catch his breath and talk about how much his life had changed in the last two weeks. He concluded by saying the most Robert thing he could say:

"But hey, I'm alive, I made it down the stairs and walked three steps to the chair."

Still, even now, he wasn't beaten. I've long disliked the idea that people 'battle' disease. Robert didn't, he embraced his diseases and worked with them, it was the situation life had dealt him and was, as always, just getting on with it.

The thing becoming clear now, however, was that Robert was coming to the end of the parameters that being cared for at home could deliver. His cough, his pain and his infection had left his condition unstable and in need of a higher level of care. Robert's needs and condition had changed, and he needed the care and support of the hospice to manage his deranged symptoms. This was a delicate conversation and there was no easy way to have it.

"I'm wondering if it's time to call the community nurse, maybe to have a few days at the hospice, it might support Robert to just get that cough and infection under control and just give you a bit of a break Maureen." I spoke quietly, compassionately. I was aware of the enormity of the words I was saying, and they were hearing. We had a brief conversation about the ward being for symptom control as well as end of life care, and that admission to the hospice wasn't necessarily the end. Maureen and Robert both agreed this was the right thing. Their community nursing team had given exceptional support to them both, and the love Robert had for the men's group meant they both trusted the hospice implicitly. I excused myself from the house briefly and called the hospice community nurse and asked her to see Robert. She advised that she would be there that afternoon. I returned and told Maureen and Robert to expect a visit from the community nurse. They were both, as always, so grateful for the care and support they received, even though anyone would forgive them a little self-pity.

"Anyway mate, that's enough about me, how are you?" asked Robert.

That was Robert all over, always looking out for others. I talked about the group, how much they missed him and, very uncharacteristically they always asked about his whereabouts and sent their best to him when he was absent. This was partly because he was just such a likeable person, but more so it seemed, that his ability to inspire, be courageous and maintain his positivity gave Robert the admiration of the group. He inspired them and showed them that this wasn't the end, that there were still things to achieve and enjoy. This impacted me too. Where previously I had felt pity for the people I supported, Robert didn't want pity. He was his own man, undeterrable, a tower of strength. He was truly fearless.

My colleagues in the community nursing team moved quickly and Robert was admitted to the ward the following day. I was keen to see him, knowing that hospice admission can be a daunting prospect and a friendly face can make such a difference. I was just on the way to pop my head round the door when I saw Maureen sitting in the hospice café. I went to speak to her. She had her daughter with her, and a half-eaten sandwich that looked like it had been half eaten for some time.

Maureen said 'Hello' to me but quickly became tearful.

"Are you on your way to see Robert?" she asked.

"Yes" I replied, "I was just going to stick my head round the door and make sure he had everything he needed".

"Would you mind going in tomorrow morning?" Maureen asked, clearly concerned at the prospect of offending me.

"He's exhausted, but he's said he'd like to see you before you do the men's group in the morning. Would you mind dropping by then?"

"Of course not" I replied, if anything privileged to have even been considered at this point.

"Tell him I'm thinking of him, and I'll see him tomorrow" I said, trying a consolatory smile. I have no idea if these are effective, but to date I've had no complaints. Maureen introduced me to one of their daughters and told me her other daughter would be travelling from London the following day.

I sat with Maureen awhile, talking about how loved Robert was and how much the chaps cared for and looked out for him. Maureen and her daughter were kind enough to share some of the wonderful things they thought about me and the men's group, always a humbling experience from somebody about to have their heart broken by circumstance. I made my excuses and left them to it but got very little work got done. I thought of Robert, who was coming to the end of a vivacious and productive, not to mention adventurous life. I thought of Maureen. Robert had made such a huge and most positive impact on my life; imagine being with him every day for over fifty years and then, him not being there anymore.

We talk a lot about not 'getting over' things but instead learning to live with them. Of all the tasks and challenges that my career had thrown up, I couldn't think of anything more harrowing, more impossible, than loving the same person for fifty years, sleeping in the same bed, laughing together, eating together, raising families, working to make a home, and then one day, being alone. Life has changed. There's a voice you've heard every day for over fifty years that you are never going to hear again. They have gone.

I couldn't empathise, I could only imagine. As Maureen sat there with her daughter contemplating the seismic shift her life was about to undertake, I walked away. I hoped that feeling some of her pain might make her feel less pain, I didn't need to be told about the futility of such a gesture. If there was anything I could have done to have been in it with her at that moment and somehow make things a little more tolerable I would have done it.

The following day was Thursday, Men's Group Day. Maureen had asked me previously to ensure the group was made aware of Robert's situation. I walked into the building, busily issuing good mornings. As I logged on to my computer I saw a flurry of activity, one message of which was inevitable, but no less shocking.

"Notification of death". I knew. In that moment, without clicking on it, I just knew.

Robert had died peacefully an hour and a half earlier. Maureen was sitting with him now. I made my way to the ward and spoke with the duty sister. Maureen had, having held vigil by Robert's bedside since admission, been convinced by family members and staff that it would be quite safe for her to pop home, change her clothes, have a shower and come back. Robert was perfectly stable, and no immediate changes were likely at that stage.

Maureen was gone little more than an hour and a half, but Robert died quietly and peacefully in solitude. I was told by the duty sister that Maureen was still by his side where she had sat since she returned to the hospice to be greeted by a sullen and distraught looking nurse who told her that Robert had died. Maureen had promised Robert she would not leave his side, and she had. They had talked about their mutual fear of him dying alone, and he had. Maureen had, through her tear-stricken eyes and panicked breaths, asked to see her regular hospice counsellor for whom it was not a working day.

"Would you like me to go and sit with her?" I asked automatically.

"I think she would appreciate that very much." was the patient response from the duty sister for whom this night shift had proved particularly challenging.

I walked into Robert's room, a privacy curtain concealed the bed from sight of the door, but audible crying could be heard. I glided silently to where Maureen was.

"Maureen, I'm so sorry" I began.

Maureen looked up with desperation, she reached for my hand and called out to me "He's dead, he's dead and I wasn't here. I promised him. I promised him I'd be here and now he's dead".

Maureen had stood loyally by Robert for over fifty years and, as she saw it, she abandoned him briefly to take a moment for herself and that was the moment his life ended. She was bereft, guilt ridden and beyond consolation or reason. I pulled up a chair and sat with Maureen. She held my hand and Robert's and sobbed with everything she had. This was a level of distress I had rarely seen in my years of working in palliative care. Maureen knew Robert was coming to the end of their life and their fifty-year union. They had rarely been apart in those times, and now, as she saw it, the definitive moment came. The test of their union, of their love, of their vows had come, and she had fallen short. I felt her pain and understood her guilt, as misplaced as it was.

I sat with Maureen for thirty or forty minutes as she cried and berated herself for the betrayal. I protested to her on her own behalf, telling her there was no way she could have known, that she had been told Robert was stable, that she could take some time out to take a break and resume her vigil. There was no reasoning and certainly no consolation. Maureen didn't just have grief, she had guilt too, and it was all I could do at this point to hope she could find it within herself to obtain inner forgiveness. Robert's pain had ended but hers had just begun.

"I just want him back", she cried burying her head into my side.

"I know", I whispered putting a hand on her shoulder. It was all I could say. I wished for some wisdom, some experience or philosophy that could make all of Maureen's pain go away. But this was it for her now. She was heartbroken, alone, and for the time being, defined by everybody including herself by her grief.

I shuffled around my seat as Maureen reached for my hand. I sat in silence as she spent her final sorrowful hours with her husband. I knew what a special man he was, how inspired I was by him, how much the men's group loved him. I knew he was irreplaceable in my world, and I had known him for the briefest of periods. I tried to calculate again how Maureen would manage being married to such a man then having nobody. I hoped that one day her heart would be healed enough to tell their stories with joyous reflection, but knew this time was far away. I knew the road that laid out in front of Maureen, and I wanted to do whatever I could to support her on her journey. I understood that grief is the price we pay for love, and the happier and more loved we are, the more people will grieve us. Maureen's despair and my sorrow were testament to a wonderful human being, but this was of no consolation to anybody at this point.

I heard a quiet knock at the door. Maureen and Robert's daughter had arrived. I felt an air of relief as I greeted her and offered condolences. This was now family time, and I had no need or desire to intrude. But I needed to say goodbye. I walked to the other side of the bed and looked to Robert. Robert was, to me, heroic. Not in the superhero or sporting champion, but more the definition given by psychologist Carol Pearson:

The hero "falls through" what is merely their life situation to discover their Real Life, which is always a much deeper river, hidden beneath the appearances. Most people confuse their life situation with their actual life, which is an underlying flow beneath everyday events. This deeper discovery is largely what religious people mean by "finding their soul."

Robert had come to the hospice for help, but ended up being a shining light to anyone he came across, be it the staff whom he made smile, the children he made laugh with his book, the men whom he inspired, and me. The gift he gave me was something I needed but would not dream of asking for- to be shown that life was indeed a gift, that our perception of what is pain and suffering and what is actual pain and suffering, are in fact, very different things. Robert showed me that courage, whilst not being the thing that cures the disease, is very much the thing that impacts how you perceive it and how you live with it. He came at a dark time for me, when I needed to be inspired, and inspire me he did; he led me into the light and life was ostensibly better for the brief time that I knew him.

In the days that followed I kept in touch with Maureen, partly because I was concerned for her welfare but also because I felt a debt of gratitude to Robert. He constantly, as I saw it, went over and above expectation to create good, I owed him this. Whilst Maureen processed her husband's death and commenced the mundane reams of paperwork that are an unwelcome accompaniment to any bereavement, she had an unexpected request for me. She was struggling to find the words for a tribute at his memorial service. Robert had, as was true to form, decided that his cremation would happen behind closed doors. He wanted to spare those who loved him from having to be there, and removed the burden of the decision, making it clear that those were his wishes and that was all there was to it.

I offered to write something. It was a country mile beyond my comfort zone, but I offered to make a few notes and just give them to Maureen to use as she saw fit. I wrote about my understanding of the word courage and how Robert had fit the bill, how he had inspired me and the group, and how there was no battle here. Robert embraced his diagnoses and made the most of them. It was heart felt, sincere and took me a matter of moments, it concluded:

On the Monday before he died, I visited Robert and Maureen at home, Robert talked of only being able to walk three steps, or to put it another way, he beamed enthusiastically' 'Hey, I walked three steps'. Robert knew he was unwell, and I think he knew his life was coming to an end, but there he was still positive, still unbeaten, and looking out for other people and reflecting on the 50 plus wonderful years he had spent with Maureen. He was so grateful for his marriage, his family and all he had, and regularly voiced it.

"But that's enough about me, how are you mate?". With all that was happening Robert was still a masterclass of compassion, class and courage. He was the best of us, and we love and miss him.

I called Maureen and arranged a time to pop over to see her. The house was no different to the one I had sat in a couple of weeks previously, still immaculate, still lovingly displayed pictures of families on holidays, graduations and weddings. I read what I had written for Maureen who asked that I change nothing and recite it at the service. I can honestly say that throughout my career I can think of no greater privilege than this. To be told that my words were enough to summarise a life, were worthy to be heard by those who loved him, for somebody like Robert was an honour.

Robert's service was, as expected, a well-attended and positive affair. The overwhelming feel of it was that we had been blessed to know this man. The emotion ran through me as I read my words, communicated how privileged I was to be welcomed there, much less to speak. The men's group also made significant efforts to attend. I said my words, sang the hymns and openly cried. I was aware my involvement had long since gone above and beyond the expectations of a social worker, that both my emotional and personal commitment had undeniably broken boundaries. I also felt this was appropriate. I left the service, briefly popped into the wake then made my excuses and left, leaving condolences and future invitations to the many who related to what I had said. I was replete with love but devoid of energy, I went home and slept.

Chapter Seventeen

Cheryl

January 2017

It was the depth of winter, that bleak part of January where Christmas is over and even the sun struggles to make it up into the sky. The post-Christmas lull weighed heavily on everyone, and the referrals continued to come thick and fast.

I was given the referral of a young man aged seventeen with a diagnosis of Asperger's. He was isolating himself since the untimely and sudden death of his father and finding life difficult to cope with. As many young people with Asperger's did, he found solace in his X-Box and the online gaming community, the global nature of which left him with a pronounced American accent even though he rarely left his bedroom in suburban middle England. He routinely talked online with peers from all over the globe. I'd seen this often enough to know it was perfectly normal and not an overt cause for concern, but I needed to meet him and try to understand how he was feeling and what support was needed.

I called his mother, a woman of 43, Cheryl, undeniably a woman of a very young age to contemplate widowhood. She was grateful for the offer of support, and I arranged to visit that afternoon.

Cheryl and her son, Jake, lived in a newbuild estate on the outskirts of town. She had enjoyed a good life, a marriage with her husband, Ian, who worked in IT had made every effort to build a home, put money aside, pay the mortgage and generally take care of things. Ian was financially buoyant enough that Cheryl's part-time administration role wasn't needed to support the upkeep of their home. Only six weeks prior to my visit, Cheryl had taken a phone call. Ian had been working in a local office where he was well known. He had a heart attack and died there and then, aged 43. Cheryl's life had spun completely off its axis as a result.

I arrived at Cheryl's house, an immaculate and leafy avenue that adequately camouflaged the misery within. The peace and quiet was a direct and clear paradox to the speed of Ian's death and the crises that befell Cheryl as a result. I rang the doorbell, one of those fancy ones with a little camera and a microphone so the householder can answer the door even if they can't answer the door.

Cheryl came to the door. She was slim with blonde hair neatly pulled back, wearing skinny jeans and an oversized Nike hoody. She had piercing blue eyes, pink cheeks and rub marks around her eyes which suggested to me she had not long been in distress. I introduced myself, Cheryl thanked me for coming and within moments we were sat in a large conservatory, on wicker furniture, drinking tea and talking about what had happened.

Cheryl needed to talk. She immediately started telling me about her love for Ian. They had met in high school and dated since the age of fifteen. Their respective families immediately got on and became friends, they got engaged aged 18 on a Valentine's Day trip to Alton Towers, they were married at the age of 21, and five years later Jake came along. Cheryl quickly offered up the unnecessary explanation that they did not want a second child. I was mildly embarrassed that she felt I needed to know this, or that I somehow thought something was amiss that they had decided not to have more children.

Cheryl explained what I already knew; that Jake was an already insular character who had retreated very much into his own space since the death of his father, spent his days going to work, coming home, then turning on his PC and

Xbox as soon as he got in, having very little voluntary human contact.

"I feel like I've failed as a mum", Cheryl whispered stifling tears.

"Tell me why", I requested.

Cheryl started to cry, quickly apologised and composed herself.

"The thing is…" Cheryl started reluctantly and pensively.

"The thing is... I've got this friend. He's been such a good friend since Ian died. He was his best mate, best men at each other's weddings, we were all at school together. The whole thing happened so quickly, he'd been so supportive since Ian died, he got divorced a few years back and he was so helpful with the funeral and everything, got me loads of photos of Ian for the service, he's just been such a good friend".

"Well, there's nothing wrong with that." I said, knowingly being naïve in the absence of all the facts. I'll have to confess here; yes, I am always genuinely concerned with the welfare of my clients and patients, but I am also a human being with an appetite for the salacious who just loves some juicy gossip. I tell you this largely to absolve myself from the guilt I feel for admitting this.

"Well, there is something wrong with that" Cheryl stated firmly.

"The day of the funeral, I was broken", Cheryl began, "Just broken. The service was lovely, so many people, faces I hadn't seen for years, people I'd forgotten, family, people we hadn't seen since we got married or since Jake was born. I was surrounded by people, it was ok, but it was a kind of purgatory knowing that after today they'd all go back to life".

"Go on", I whispered, suddenly feeling a little less than congruent about both wanting to be supportive but fascinated by the story.

"We all went to the World's End after the wake, me and all the lads Ian played rugby with and a few others from the funeral. The more I drank, the more people left and before you know it, we're getting together in the pub", Cheryl took a breath "in the fucking pub toilet", she announced face filling with shame, voice stuttering with torment.

"I don't know why. I just saw everybody leaving and suddenly it was real. I was so alone. People had been staying at home with me to make sure I was ok and suddenly it was the night of my husband's funeral, and I knew I was going to be alone for the first night in thirty years. I had never felt so alone, so scared, so low."

"The love of my life, the only man I'd ever been with, the father of my child, his family" Cheryl stuttered, "his family took me as one of their own", Cheryl was now crying without restraint.

"He was my everything. We did everything together. He was dead three weeks, and I betrayed him and everything we were".

My primary thought was Carl Rogers, unconditional positive regard, judge not lest ye be judged, the four pillars of AA, don't take anything personally, do your best and, integrally do not make assumptions. I had no point of reference for somebody in Cheryl's position. She had kept one relationship her entire adult life and within weeks of his death she had slept with his best friend. I could quickly see the hurt and shame in her eyes.

"It suddenly dawned on me that Ian's family were nothing to me anymore, I was their dead boy's wife, nothing more, not a blood relative, nothing. Then. Then I got pissed slept with his best mate, dated him for three weeks and split up from him. I feel dirty. Everything I was I gave to him. My wedding vows, I gave it all up so easily". Cheryl wasn't just grieving the death of her husband; she was remorseful that what she saw as the duty of a grieving widow was a task so utterly beyond her. She had fallen at the first hurdle. She knew people were judging her. Ian's family were devastated at what they saw as their daughter in law taking a matter of weeks to move on from their son's death, but on that cold, drunk, lonely night, Cheryl saw her actions as a desperate final gasp at closeness with Ian. This had gone horribly wrong.

"I lost the right to be his widow when I went with somebody else" Cheryl stated directly. I understood this totally. For her whole adult life, she had been in a relationship with one man, now, as Cheryl saw it, it wasn't even her most recent relationship. She felt she had, by having a short affair, lost her right to grieve and betrayed her husband, losing his family in the process. As discussed, for a man in recovery as I was at this stage, the four agreements include not assuming anything. As a professional, judgment is neither needed nor useful. I could see Cheryl's pain as she spoke. She was remorseful and lost. She thought the void left by her husband's death could be filled quickly, and in a mess of drunken desperation and grief she sought out connection to ease the hurt. In doing so she had made everything worse for herself.

Cheryl talked a while longer. I was becoming aware that her son whom I had initially come to see hadn't been discussed. I immediately acknowledged this when it came to me, and I arranged to see him another time. Cheryl confessed that her son was acting in the way he always had and that in reality, the referral for support for him was a desperate bid to talk to somebody, anybody who would listen, validate, and more than anything: not judge. Not understanding a situation rarely prevents judgement from many people. Cheryl knew this and knew the in the eyes of many she had gone from the young, grieving widow to the remorseless, scarlet woman who betrayed the love of her life as soon as his body turned cold.

I felt for Cheryl. Her grief was fast becoming disenfranchised because of her actions and how people were feeling about it. I understood that what appeared was a desperate grab for connection had gone badly wrong and now Cheryl was left with the definitive hangover. I explained to Cheryl what I thought had happened and why she had done what she had done. She presented as relieved that I had tried to empathise rather than just judge. I told her that, unless a person had walked a mile in her shoes, they were in no place to make judgements or draw conclusions without knowing all the facts.

The problem for Cheryl remained. Ian's family were grieving too, they had seen Cheryl as a connection to their son, as a living reminder, as family. They were now bereft of compassion for her, they didn't understand how she could have done what she did, with his best friend whom they also loved. I was struggling to understand this too, but I didn't have to understand, I just needed to listen without judgement. What was becoming clear was that Cheryl's grief was complicated by her guilt and feelings of self-loathing. Our session was coming to a close, but I promised to see Cheryl the following week to talk more and see what services I could offer to support her to recover and move forward. Cheryl thanked me and walked me to the front door. I left her alone in the house and went back to my car.

I was overwhelmed with compassion for Cheryl. She hadn't asked for any of this. She had been happily married in the same relationship since childhood, she had relied on Ian, loved him unconditionally, raised his child while he earned the money to keep them well, and now she was adrift. She had only ever functioned as an adult with Ian and was without the basic skills to manage without him. While she coped in the only way she knew how, she ended up hurting those close to her and hurting herself. To heal and learn to live, Cheryl needed forgiveness from those she had hurt, but first she had to forgive herself.

I couldn't sleep for worrying about Cheryl. I understood what she had done, and I understood why Ian's family had ceased contact and had no interest in forgiving her. I knew from my own experiences how the extremes of loneliness could provoke disastrous decision making, usually starting with heavy drinking and going from there. There were no winners here. I understood why Cheryl did what she did, and I understood why so many were let down and heartbroken by her actions. It was just the most incredibly sad situation. A family literally torn apart by grief and its consequences.

The following week I went to Cheryl's house as agreed. There was no answer at the door. I called her mobile, no reply from that either. As the weeks went by, I attempted to call Cheryl a few more times but she declined to take my calls. I cared and worried for her welfare but reflected that, if there was one thing Cheryl wanted to communicate to me, it was that's she did not want to communicate with me.

The following day I saw her walking hand in hand with a man as I was driving to a visit, she didn't look overly happy but neither did she look ill at ease or uncomfortable. The relief for me was that I knew she was safe and as ok as she could be.

I wasn't sure if the man she was with was the man we had been talking about, Ian's best friend, but I took this as confirmation that whatever emotions she had communicated to me, she wasn't wanting to move forward with it at this stage. Not taking these things as personal is integral to resilience in palliative care social work. Maybe I could have done things better, maybe Cheryl needed to open her heart to somebody then never speak to them again, I wasn't sure. One thing I was certain of was that Cheryl's journey through grief would undoubtedly be disruptive and complex, but she had made the choice to go through this journey without my help. I even sent her a text telling her I could arrange a different worker to support her if that would be better for her, she didn't respond. I ensured she knew that when she was ready to talk, I, or one of my colleagues, would be ready to listen.

I sincerely hoped Cheryl would find happiness without my support, and correctly predicted I would never hear from her again.

Chapter Eighteen

Amanda

January 2018

In 2010 I left a job I'd very long been happy and content in, to go and work in a care home for Autistic children as part of their management team. A friend of mine was the senior manager and spent long hours telling me what a great team we would make, and what an ambitious and forward-thinking organisation this was. He walked out of the job five months later. He took a week's annual leave without bothering to tell anybody, on his return, he logged on to his work emails and upon seeing the varying levels of chaos, unfinished tasks and general incompetence that ensued in his absence, and all clearly his fault, he quit on the spot, returning only to hand in his keys and work phone. The final rusty nail in this rather heavy and undesirable coffin is that he took a job at the place I had previously vacated on his recommendation.

So, I was left to be managed by Amanda Kelley. Amanda Kelley was one of the most homophobic, manipulative, racist and ill-tempered humans I have ever encountered. I took an immediate dislike to her, partly because she flatly refused to remember anybody's name calling them either

Fanny or Albert, but also because she decided for no apparent reason that I was gay and should therefore be subject to an ongoing and significant campaign of homophobic abuse. I had come from a working environment where I was respected and valued and had never dreamed that such an experience could happen to me. It knocked me sideways. Was this real?

There then followed a sinister campaign in every meeting with the directors whereby my experience and qualifications were called into question, especially in comparison to an acquaintance of hers called simply 'Miss Jones'. Amanda routinely lied about her relationship with Miss Jones, firstly stating they were work colleagues, then friends, then people who lived in the same town, then the same estate, then the same building, then the same home. Soon enough, as Amanda taunted, berated and manipulated her way through meetings, a role in the management team was made for Miss Jones and their tyrannical and bullying culture spread through the organisation leading to rafts of resignations from staff, including after two years of employment, mine.

By the end of my two-year run with the organisation, my self-esteem was shot, so I took a new job on the other side of the county nearer home. Amanda had successfully manipulated the directors into thinking she was an asset, but her ludicrous and often unfeasible lies made the workplace a laughingstock. On one occasion she claimed the office had a phone call from the fraud squad about a service user accessing a Mobility car illegally. This seemed fairly feasible until, upon some questioning from the directors she panicked and announced that the fraud squad officers name was John Fraud. She also claimed ownership of a care home, a management consultancy, a firearm, a grandfather in the IRA, the ability to talk a suicidal teenager off a bridge (the location, time, details of the teenager and any other further details were not forthcoming when asked by the directors why she had been late for work). She also used a dognapping as an excuse for lateness on another occasion.

Eventually I found alternative employment running a small care home for a charity nearer home in Hereford. I bid an insincere farewell to Amanda, and deleted any emails and text messages, hoping that I would never see, hear from or think of her again.

A few weeks after I had started in my new role, a colleague from Amanda's service emailed me asking for a job, I went through the motions, Emma was successful in her application and was part of our new team within a couple of weeks. I thought my awful two years in Amanda Kelley's grip was over, I had left her behind.

The phone rang. It was my new regional manager asking me to come to the office at once. It was a mile down the road, so I drove down straight away. The office was a picture of bleakness, building contractors, cider factories, and brick built 1970's office blocks in front of a backdrop of the smell of mass-fried chicken from the nearby Cargon works, a unique and appalling smell that you'd have to go to Hereford to experience.

I made my way into a deserted office, passed the sink on a rotten wooden platform generously known as The Kitchen, and into the office. There were two desks, lots of ring binders, a photocopier and the smell of dust, instant coffee and gone off milk. My manager, Leanne, and the HR manager Debbie were awaiting my arrival. I greeted them in a friendly but professional manner. This was not reciprocated.

A chair had been set out for me to sit on, whilst Leanne and Debbie sat facing me. Leanne was slim, around six-foot-tall, an accomplished distance runner and healthy eater.

Debbie was pushing retirement in a burgundy trouser suit and Margaret Thatcher hair. Her face could be kind, but it wasn't today.

"We've had a report, we need to ask you some questions."

"Fire away" I responded with suspicion. I had rather hoped that I'd left drama and psychological chicanery behind.

"The report has been made anonymously. It is suggesting that you are in a sexual relationship with Emma, who you recommended for the job, and we have recruited" as if I didn't know or had forgotten.

As soon as the words came, I was in no surprise or doubt as to what had happened here. I had left her control and now Amanda wanted one last dig in my ribs, one last kick. I had hated her when we worked together but now, I had planned to think nothing of her at all. She had scuppered my plans.

"Out of the question. Absolutely not. No." I replied.

"Well,", said Leanne clearly disbelieving me and clearly furious about the situation: "We now have to redeploy her, you won't be able to work together, she'll have to work in one of the other homes".

"OK" I replied, shaking my head in disbelief. Nobody seemed to entertain the possibility that this was some sort of stitch up.

I left the office in a bubble of confusion and anger. For fucks sake. Why would somebody do that? I've left. She spent two years trying to make me leave and now I've left she's still putting the boot in. I just couldn't understand her mindset at all. It transpired that Emma had had a very public and unpleasant exchange of words with Amanda before she had left, so it made sense she would want to throw both of us under a bus. I denied the charges and vowed to get on with my life and my job and just move on, hoping that Amanda would too.

I had just started a new relationship, this has since become a marriage, and was asleep that night with my girlfriend when I was woken by my phone.

"Hello?" a male voice stuttered on the other end. "I, err, I got your number from a forum, and well, I was wondering if you'd like to meet up. We have a lot in common". I was half asleep and in no mood for whatever practical joke somebody was playing.

"I don't know what you're talking about mate, you've got the wrong number. Bye." I said before abruptly hanging up and switching my phone off.

Rebecca didn't wake thankfully. This sounded ominous and I really didn't want to be answering questions about dodgy people off forums calling late at night because we 'had a lot in common' to a woman I was quickly falling in love with so early in a relationship.

The following day two more text messages came through, one simply saying: "I got your number from the forum, if you're still around and still up for it, give me a call." Another said: "I think we could help each other out, text me if you're still willing".

The text messages and late-night calls became more frequent. My best guess was that somebody had put my name and details on some sort of dogging or fetish forum or something similar. I've no problem with such activities, I'd acted in ways that challenged social values frequently, usually after alcohol, 'each to their own' I thought. I gradually went about blocking numbers that sent me messages or tried to contact me. As the calls became more frequent, I began to lose patience. The red flag I painfully missed was that every call appeared to be from men.

"Wrong number", "Not interested" and latterly "Fuck off" became my responses.

I decided to come clean to Rebecca and tell her what was going on. She presented as slightly agitated that, in such a new relationship, the unwelcome sight of drama and nonsense had reared its head. I told her I had no idea who was doing it, or where my name had been posted and why, but my best guess was that, for a joke, somebody had put my name and number on a forum somewhere. She was happy with my explanation and appreciated my honesty. I was working a night shift that evening across county and set off for work. I was about half an hour into an hour-long journey when I received a text message from Rebecca. I saw the preview on my phone as I sat at a red light.

"I really need to speak to you, call me as soon as you can".

As a rule, such messages are rarely preparation for good news, so I found a layby and pulled over. Whoever had taken the time out to call my employer and make accusations against me had taken their vendetta to the next level.

I called Rebecca. She answered the call with a quick 'hello', the conversation then escalated quickly with a follow up question:

"Have you ever tried to kill yourself?"

"No." I blurted out without even considering what circumstances had pre-empted such a question.

"Never." I said by way of cementing my commitment to my truth.

"What's happened?" I asked. I was spooked, but what Rebecca told me rocketed me into a stratosphere of discomfort, distress, suspicion, fear and total and absolute mistrust of anyone and everyone.

"Well…", Rebecca began, clearly distressed herself and fearing the worst: "After all those calls and text messages you got, saying people were trying to contact you after seeing your details on a forum, I googled your phone number and your first name and I've found the forum your name has been posted on."

"Ok", I said. I was wary that maybe this truth wasn't something I was ready to hear just before a night shift, but I wanted to know what Rebecca knew. I was paranoid and fearful, and I was going to be away from home over night. I needed to know she was safe.

"What is it?".

"It's a suicide pact forum" Rebecca said. She sounded terrified.

"A. What? What? I just. What?" the word 'speechless' is overused in common parlance, but here I was, stuttering, stammering and lost for words. More than anything I wanted to skip work, go back home and be with Rebecca. The thought of her being alone for the night at home sickened me. I was lost, my stomach churned, I considered every eventuality, was it my ex-wife? Somebody with a grudge? A practical joke? Then it occurred to me. Amanda.

The forum was for people who wanted to die by suicide but wanted to find somebody else who wanted to die in the same way, so they could support each other and die together. I thought about the calls, the loneliness of those who gained the courage to text or call me only to be told to 'fuck off', or recognise that, in their darkest hour, they were the victim of a practical joke. Those poor people werre desperate, alone, suicidal, and at their lowest moment. At the pit of everything that had brought them to draw the conclusion that suicide was the answer, they found me, unwilling to help, not understanding and devoid of all empathy. I took a moment, my heart was beating fast and heavy, my brow sweating, my mouth watering like it does just before you throw up.

"What does it say?" I asked.

"It was 'hi, my name is Andy', it says you're a 37-year-old man and it says that you're in Hereford and it says that you're ready to kill yourself and want people to help you do it".

Silence.

Even now, after years of reflection, and still no clarity over who had done this and why, I was devoid of enquiry. The who's and why's, the how's, all eluded me. I was numb, adrenaline coursing through every fragment of my being and my bones, I assured Rebecca this was a practical joke gone wrong, that it wasn't me, that I was fine, but I was confused and hurt.

I ended the call with Rebecca and drove the rest of my journey to my night shift, a one-to-one care provision in rural Herefordshire. The shift went slowly, I cleaned, tidied, sweated, counted money tins, completed medication audits, ensured the food records were up to date, but nothing could cleanse my soul or clear my mind. I had no proof it was Amanda, nor have I ever received any. The only saving grace of Rebecca's sickening revelation was that now I was able to support and take care of those who found my number on the forum and contacted me. I was able to tell them to get help, that they were worthy of love, that maybe these feelings may pass. I'll never know if it made a difference, or if anybody took notice of my responses. There is far too much uncertainty in this story, but time was the only thing that allowed me to heal from the experience.

In my mind I had concluded it was Amanda, and I hated her for it.

I decided to involve the Police and quickly wished I hadn't. I was informed that no crime had been committed, and that as the forum had no admin or moderation, nobody could take responsibility for, or delete the posting of my details on the forum. It was at this point I was considering the possibility that the universe had taken a dislike to me and maybe this was just how life was going to be now. I decided there and then to change my phone number, texting a few trusted and loyal friends to advise them of my new one, and disappeared from social media which, slightly to my disappointment, only one person noticed.

The text messages and calls came to an end, and I left my job to undertake my social work degree, still my best ever decision. I found a place to call home with Rebecca, nobody knew where I lived, how to contact me or where I was working. I had completed my chapter with Amanda.

Eight years later....

"No". I froze. The day hospice handover meeting was not a place that normally provoked any kind of response in me, the team were lovely but rarely needed my input, so my attendance at their morning meeting usually consisted of me bidding everybody good morning and sitting checking tasks and emails on my laptop just in case my intervention was needed. A widescreen TV on the wall displayed a list of the day's patients.

Amanda's name was on the patient list of people coming in that day. The screen showed a date of birth and first line of address. I didn't know where she lived, but the date of birth seemed consistent with hers. Then the professional conversation came, nurses, a doctor, physios, occupational therapists and care assistants discussed the patient.

"Lady who runs care homes", Check.

"Morbidly obese", Check.

"Bullying, rude and quite obnoxious at times", Check.

It was her. She was ill, coming to the end of her life, she was no longer a threat to me. Realistically she was never really a threat to me anyway, but she occupied a place in my psyche. She tapped into my vulnerability, saw my flaws, knew my insecurities and exploited them. Amanda the person, and Amanda the enemy I had conjured up within were different people. In my head she was still that person. In reality, she was a patient who needed help.

I had no desire to dig up the past, but I was also certain that if Amanda saw me, she would feel ill-at-ease and reluctant to engage. As much as Amanda had sought to make my life awful, she was still a patient. I went to speak with the day hospice manager and advised her that Amanda and I had worked together and that it probably wasn't appropriate for me to support her in any way. This was partly because I didn't want to see her, but also because I found myself starting to feel compassionate towards her. She was coming into the hospice for the first time, which was challenging enough without seeing somebody whom you knew you had made life extremely difficult for. The day hospice manager agreed, concluding that if Amanda needed anything they would deploy one of my colleagues from another department.

Within an hour I had received a call asking me to go down to day hospice to see a different patient about an enquiry regarding housing. I knew what this meant. I walked down the stairs and through the entrance of day hospice. I continued through the corridor into the main room where the patients were. I came to the door, looked in and, through all the patients, staff and bustle, my eyes applied tunnel vision towards Amanda, sitting in a reclining chair in the far corner of the room. I felt sick. The memories of the suicide calls, the abuse, the yelling, the manipulation, all fermented into a heavy stomach and weak legs. It was time.

I walked over to where she was after indicating to the nurse, I would see the patient they had called me about in a moment.

"Oh my God, Amanda?" I said gesticulating surprise with a hand over my mouth.

She had lost a lot of weight, her once flamboyantly dyed hair was now grey, and her booming voice croaky and laboured.

"Well, well, well" she cleared her throat. "Hello stranger, what are you doing here?".

"I requalified a few years ago, been here as a social worker for a couple of years now" I replied. Social norms require we should have asked about each other's health at this point. I treaded carefully.

"It's good to see you" I offered gently, "how come you're here?" an awkwardly worded question, but Amanda's unexpected and unwelcome return to my existence had knocked me. Amanda explained that she was suffering from an aggressive form of pancreatic cancer. Her prognosis was poor, she didn't have long to live, months if she was lucky.

We talked for a short while, mainly about what a compassionate and magnificent organisation the hospice was, very little about her work or the home we were colleagues at. As we talked politely it became clear that Amanda's treatment of me was far more significant in my eyes than hers. I advised her that if she needed a social worker for advice or support, I would ensure a colleague, not me, would be there to support her. I didn't want to make things awkward for her, talking to somebody she knew when she would be better off talking to a stranger.

The real Amanda was fading before my very eyes. She was no longer the person who tried to undermine and humiliate me, she was a patient, fearful of her disease, fearful of death and no longer a threat to me. It occurred to me that I had built her up in my mind to be far greater than the sum of her parts. I was desperate to ask her why she had behaved in the way she did, if she received any advantage from making my life so difficult, but this was neither the time nor the place. Those memories were my problem, she had far greater things to worry about. I told Amanda I had enjoyed seeing her again and wished her well. She smiled with what looked like sincerity. A few weeks later Amanda was admitted to the ward at the hospice for end-of-life care and died peacefully surrounded by those who loved her.

The day after a patient dies, a hospice social worker will meet with a family member to talk them through next steps for the family, how to arrange emotional support, how to book a funeral, how to register a death, let the relevant agencies know, all of the things that can catch you unawares if you're not ready for them. It is also the time that the family members collect any belongings that the patient had with them when they died.

In the absence of any other social worker on site that day, I was going to meet with Amanda's family. Her mum and dad were coming in. The thought of meeting them exhausted me. I secretly hoped for some personal resolution as to why she had behaved how she did, or some justification that explained her character and her actions. I took the short walk from the office to where Amanda's parents were sitting in reception. I walked to them, the only people sitting in the area, and confirmed who they were. I asked them to follow me, and we walked to the office together. Amanda's mum and dad sat in the two armchairs in the window overlooking the carpark. I sat on a plastic office swivel chair with my hands in my lap introducing myself and the purpose of the meeting.

Amanda's mum was delightful, polite, and did all the talking. She was around seventy, dressed in a long, colourful flowery dress, she introduced herself as Sheila, and her husband as Dennis. Sheila wore subtle make up with blonde but greying hair. She had a kind smile that denied her grief. Dennis was of similar age. He had dark grey hair slicked back, hadn't shaved in a few days and wore jeans and a black donkey jacket. For the duration of the pleasantries, he sat in silence.

Sheila told me how Amanda was an only child, that they had wanted more children, but it had never happened. She told me how Amanda had thrived at school through academia. I forgot all that I knew about Amanda and immersed myself in the grief of those who shared this moment with me. Sheila was grateful for the care and support Amanda had received.

"We were so grateful for the hospice" she said in a half whisper. "It was nice that she knew you too, you worked together, didn't you?" I didn't know she knew, and I had no desire to raise it.

"We did yes, at The Ryan Hillman Residential Trust" I said, gently, with a smile that suggested happy memories.

"She wasn't everyone's cup of tea" Sheila said, almost by way of explanation.

"She was a great manager" I replied, "We worked together at a time when I was finding things very difficult, and she treated me decently".

Sheila smiled, "Thankyou".

We all stood without a word confirming the closure of the meeting, as we did, I offered my hand to Dennis who had said nothing. I looked into his eyes and saw a level of sorrow I had rarely encountered in this saddest of places. It was the one and only time that I have done this:

"Come here" I said holding out my arms. Dennis stumbled, threw his arms around me and sobbed. He sobbed relentlessly and breathlessly. His head pressed into my chest, within moments I could feel warm breath and tears soaking through my shirt. He struggled to control his breathing as his tears and grief took him over. I supported Dennis to sit in the chair I had just vacated, went down on one knee and held his hand. He attempted to speak, but every time he did another wave of anguish overcame him.

"This has been coming", said Sheila with an unnecessary apologetic tone. "This is the first time he's cried". Minutes passed, Sheila and I helped Dennis to his feet. He attempted to say 'thank you' but ended up just mouthing the words as another Tsunami of tears fought its way out of him. Sheila thanked me, took her husband by the arm, and left. Amanda's pain was ending while her parent's pain was just beginning. As I watched them walk awkwardly arm in arm across the car park they stopped and held each other, not ready to leave, not ready to say goodbye, not ready to undertake the practicality of registering a death, calling family members, planning a funeral. They were good people on a journey they had not chosen to go on. I wished good things for them and empathy from those who surrounded them. All three of us were laying Amanda to rest.

Epilogue

So, our time together is nearly over for now, dear reader. I have made myself vulnerable and declared to the world that I have stories to tell and the self-belief to sit down and write them. I have tried unsuccessfully to convince myself that if this book goes unpublished and unread, then the cathartic nature of writing it will still have made the cause worthwhile. We both know that this isn't true.

As I write this, March 2024 is ending. The UK is currently the most conflicted and angry I can ever remember it being. The NHS is under attack for wanting a fair working wage, many continue to dispute the evidence over whether Covid was real or not, eight years after the Brexit vote, radio talk shows invite people to argue the toss over the phones like some sort of perverse anti-intellectual coliseum, racists in the Conservative Party really don't seem to need to deny being racist anymore and we seem to have a government that thinks everybody will buy the idea that people trying to access the country on small boats are the reason food bank use is at an all-time high, and the cost of living has exploded through their rented roofs.

Yet through all this conflict, this disagreement, this 'I'm right, you're wrong, fuck you' nature of discourse, there is humanity and love on every corner. There are stories of courage, bravery and kindness that will forever warm your soul if you just allow yourself to hear them with an open mind and an open heart.

I have met and worked with people who found generosity of spirit, kind words and empathy when they would have been forgiven for allowing their pain to take over their good nature and snap back, cut themselves off, or just disappear into a cloud of bitterness and blame.

For every story of hate I can tell you five of love, for every story of indifference I can tell you five of compassion, empathy and vulnerability. For every story of revenge, I can tell you five about kindness, of people that care for others selflessly and with little or no gain for themselves.

We may have a provocative and divisive media that seeks to set young against old, transgender against cis, gay people against heterosexual, men against women, those who work against those who are unable to, but here is the truth; Nobody goes to their grave thinking about things like that. No family sits at the bed of a family member when they are coming to the end of life and separates into sides based on sexual preference or political leaning. At the hospice we haven't had many people announce a change of heart on

Brexit or an electoral vote with their final breath. They have more important considerations.

People want to say 'I love you', sometimes they say 'I'm sorry', sometimes they say 'thank you', but at that time of life instinct takes over, and our instinct is to be close to those we love, to show compassion and understanding to those we've disagreed with, and to be kind enough to forgive ourselves when we get things wrong, make mistakes or just don't know.

I can remember very clearly supporting a bereaved young man, his mother was angry that the hospice gates were not working, that somebody had told her to be there at the wrong time, that there were not enough spaces in the car park. When I asked her if she was ok, she burst into tears, not because the day had gone so badly, but because:

"I can't remember the last time somebody asked me that".

It would have been the easiest thing in the world to walk away, shout back or argue, but something in this lady's manner, maybe the tone of her voice, maybe the agitation at such seemingly small things, showed me that more than anything she needed compassion. She was alone with her disabled son, her husband had died, which meant significant financial distress as she was a full-time carer.

She had to move home as a result and her son would therefore most likely end up moving in to care as she would now have to work full- time. The death had been the start of a chain reaction of misfortune that had led her to my door. I'm not telling you this for any kind of self-congratulation. I am telling you because we need to understand that every behaviour is a form of communication, that behind every yelled expletive, every road rage, every letter of complaint, there might just be a voice that just desperately needs to be heard, a bereaved soul desperate for validation, or just somebody who is crying for help. Everybody is trying to find their way, to get by, figure out a purpose and an identity. I sincerely hope that if this book has showed you anything, it is that empathy and compassion can only make the world a better place, even if we are provoked, angry or hurt. That is why we come to work here every day and do what we do, it's not a chore it's a privilege.

To end as we began:

"Far and away the best prize that life offers is the chance to work hard at work worth doing".

Afterword- A morning in therapy

"So anyway, I made a critical error, I allowed myself to like them". I was starting on what I can only describe as a reflective rant about why I was struggling with clients, and how two families were keeping me up at night.

After the Noel debacle, I waited eighteen months then found Richard, a therapist who looked like a therapist, talked like a therapist, and had a room that told me he was a therapist, full of counselling and psychology books he had read and understood.

Richard, being a therapist that sees therapists can smell bullshit a mile off.

"It's not ok to like your clients?" he asked inquisitively.

"Well," I stuttered, "It is, but, I mean, you know, boundaries".

It occurred to me I'd been kidding myself about this for a good long while. In pursuit of professionalism and boundaries, I'd inadvertently broken the biggest boundary of all. Richard was like a dog with a bone, he listened to me stutter then launched the killer blow.

"Is it ok to love your clients?"

Oh god, stomach churning, cheeks reddening, here come the tears.

"I… oh god I'm going to cry in a moment. I feel like I've treated them with love. Like. I mean. I've done eulogies for people I've supported; I've called them to check in and make sure they're ok, I text on anniversaries sometimes. I've treated them with love. But then…" I was thinking aloud by this stage; my words were as surprising to me as they were to Richard.

"I've heard your words, I've heard you speak about the people you support" said Richard, "and when I hear your words, I hear love" He said.

Tears.

"It's overwhelming sometimes." I said between sniffs and sighs and gasps. "I've got this family now. I'm supporting their son. Well, I'm supposed to be supporting their son but I'm supporting them too. They're the nicest people. I mean the nicest, loveliest, kindest people. They've taken their elder son to the hospital at Christmas. He's been discharged. They can find nothing wrong with him. And he, he".

I was manic now. I thought I was ok all this time but I wasn't. The floodgates are open and I wasn't sure when they'd be closing again.

"He died in the car. Minutes after discharge. Fourteen. Fourfuckingteen. Why him? Why them? Why not me? Why not anyone? It just seems so fucking unfair, and it would be so much easier for me if I didn't care about them, and I wasn't emotionally involved".

I sighed again. I breathed deeply, picturing a military PT officer yelling "Compose yourself. Control your breathing". Oh, this was boot camp alright.

I needed to deflect. I felt things I didn't know I felt.

"What do you think?" I asked. My therapist often knew how to surprise me, to escort me to the edge of where I think I am going, then change direction and reveal a side of myself I didn't even know existed.

"I love all my clients unconditionally. I pray for them. I just can't be friends with them". How a sentence could be so riddled with oxymoron yet make such perfect sense summarised his genius.

"Fucking hell that's it isn't it?". I sighed, threw my head back and realised what I hadn't realised before. I couldn't do this job without love. I couldn't work effectively, be true to myself, give of myself, make myself vulnerable without love. It just wouldn't work. Maybe that's why my wife often told me that she felt I was empty at the end of the working day, that the hospice got the best of me.

I'd turned a corner. It all made sense now. But my god did I need some sleep.

At some point I acknowledged that I would have to dig very deep to understand this. It made me feel so much better about everything. I would never want my interventions to be clinical or mechanical, but the idea that there could be love for clients whilst maintaining boundaries was new, and more importantly, enlightening to me.

Perhaps the mental health crash that had led me into these sessions of therapy was some impact of stifled emotion. It was clear I had been affected by much of the trauma I had experienced, particularly after the time of Covid, but then it happened upon me. We know stifling and burying trauma, adverse experiences, sorrow and remorse is bad for us, and we all do it. This is why therapy, emotional support and counselling is so needed and why the mental health agenda is so essential. However, Brenee Brown tells us if we numb vulnerability and shame, and the things that make us vulnerable and shamed, then we also numb the positive emotions like joy, happiness, love and excitement. It was becoming evident that stifling or burying love had become problematic. This was where palliative care social work disappeared on a tangent from, for example, adult services social work. You could easily offer a systemic or process led service to people there, assess, support plan, review, repeat, but this job needed emotional connection, use of self, to give of myself. I had to feel to work effectively and honestly.

Suddenly there was a maelstrom of emotions, reflections and discoveries. This was why I felt anger towards a man who died by suicide rather than picking his children up from a party. I know about mental health, I know about suicide prevention, and yet I couldn't feel sympathy for him, only anger that he abandoned his children. This is why I felt such emptiness when I left every session I did with a family whose father had died very suddenly, leaving a mum to raise two teenage daughters. Their emptiness was my emptiness. I found myself feeling guilty about going home to my wife, daughter and cats knowing that was all I needed to bring me contentment, knowing full well that their contentment had been taken from them.

If grief is the price we pay for love, then it makes perfect sense that I would crash mentally. I wanted to heal the hurt and fix the heartbreak of every person I supported. I wanted to commit to love, cure the disease, solve the problems, absolve the wrongdoings and make everything right where it was wrong. It's no wonder these revelations caused such exhaustion. This empty feeling had been fermenting within me for too long.

"How do you feel?" my Richard asked.

"Fucking hell" was the best I could do.

"I think I need a sleep".

"Please tell me you're not doing any face-to-face work for a few hours" he said gently but assertively.

"Not 'til this afternoon" I replied, relieved I could give him the correct response.

It was like the feeling of not being in pain any more after a migraine, the sense of acid relief after the vomit you knew was coming, of getting your breath back after an intense gym session, all in one. But relief. Oh, the relief. I suddenly felt like I'd had an epiphany and could maybe get on with life and enjoy things again without having to remind myself of mine and my loved one's mortality. The Inner

Monologue Goblin sat in his cottage with the full pipe and slippers, feet up, nodding his approval and eyeing me warmly over the spectacles that were perched on the end of his beaky nose.

It was the breakthrough that saved, if not my sanity, then certainly my career. I thanked Richard; he walked me to the door, and I went to my car. It was a beautiful day, blue sky, as warm as it needed to be, and I now had a countryside drive to reflect on what I had learned about myself. The bright sunshine filtered through the dust and grit on the windscreen, so I stopped and filled up the washer at the garage. It was a very long time since I'd done this. Mundane tasks no longer seemed mundane, my purpose and enthusiasm were back with me. I had turned a corner.

Acknowledgments, Thanks and Love

Rebecca- For editing, advising, listening and designing. Thankyou!

Mum and Dad- Cheers for that.

Bert- "From being nearly dead, you've learned how to be alive".

Breeny, Lou, Sally, Jo and Pammy (I hope your ex-husband's anus never recovers).

Sarah PH, I do not know where to start, a guiding light always, thank you.

Rebecka, for spotting my mistakes before I even made them, thank you.

Sheena- thank you for the proofread and feedback.

Claire G- Always grateful for your support.

Debbie W- Thank you for laughing at the funny bits and crying at the sad bits.

The Big Staceys.

Jason Williamson.

Howard B- For successful and effective Goblin management.

Stu Jones and Bads for all things audio and studio related- cheers lads!

Punch, Davies, Pallett, Twm and Tonto.

To Caroline, James, Stanley and George, with love.

Vic and Bill, I nicked your surname, hope you don't mind x.

Emma K, thank you for listening and the lovely encouragement.

Simon Hall and the BCU team

Steve at Whitehouse- You're gonna LEARN today.

MLB Friday 0715

Printed in Great Britain
by Amazon